talk
WITH
teens

about feelings, family, relationships, and the future

50
Guided Discussions for
School and Counseling Groups

A companion to
talk with teens about self and stress

jean sunde peterson, ph.d.

edited by pamela espeland

free spirit **Works for kids™**
PUBLISHING®

Library of Congress Cataloging-in-Publication Data
Peterson, Jean Sunde, 1941–
        Talk with teens about feelings, family, relationships, and the future :
    50 guided discussions for school and counseling groups / Jean Sunde
    Peterson ; edited by Pamela Espeland.
            p.   cm.
        "A companion to Talk with teens about self and stress."
        Includes bibliographical references and index.
        ISBN 0-915793-88-1 (trade paper : alk. paper)
            1. Counseling in secondary education—United States. 2. Discussion.
    3. Teacher participation in educational counseling—United States.
    4. Emotions. 5. Interpersonal relations—United States. 6. Youth—United
    States—Attitudes. I. Espeland, Pamela, 1951–   . II. Peterson, Jean
    Sunde, 1941–   Talk with teens about self and stress. III. Title.
    LB1620.5.P446   1995
    373.14'6—dc20   95-13024
                                                                        CIP

Cover and book design by MacLean & Tuminelly
Cover photograph by Marc Scholtes
Index prepared by Eileen Quam and Theresa Wolner

10 9 8 7 6 5 4
Printed in the United States of America

Free Spirit Publishing Inc.
400 First Avenue North, Suite 616
Minneapolis, MN 55401
(612) 338-2068

dedication

To family, colleagues,
mentors, students,
and friends who have taught me—
in relationship.

acknowledgments

I continue to learn and am grateful for those who teach me, both formally and informally. Just as I did for *Talk with Teens about Self and Stress,* I want to acknowledge Jack Lauer and Fred Stephens, two South Dakota principals who gave me the kind of autonomy as a teacher that fostered experimentation. The many discussion groups I led at Lincoln High School in Sioux Falls were, of course, the result of that kind of encouragement, and they also provided a wealth of experiences to draw from for this volume. The thousands of writing assignments my students submitted during my years as a high school English teacher also were a rich resource. Long-term friends Norma Haan and Loila Hunking continue to stimulate thinking and to put thought-provoking literature into my hands. In recent student years, an array of mentors and friends, including Volker Thomas, Ann Ellsworth, and Joanne Daggit have contributed informally to many of the strands that are included in this volume. And, certainly not least important, there is the powerful impact of my parents, siblings, husband Reuben, daughter Sonia, and son Nathan in this regard as well.

Pamela Espeland, my editor and colleague in both this project and the first volume of *Talk with Teens,* has provided the kind of challenge and guidance that, in the end, produces clarity of both purpose and content. The success of that first volume attests to the value of collaboration and debate in creating a complex work that can be applied to a multitude of situations.

Early in my teaching career, I began regularly to attend workshops, conferences, and in-service sessions dealing with affective concerns. I took notes, kept files on various topics, consulted with counselors and other mental health professionals, and read books. I am grateful for those experiences. When I began the discussion groups in Sioux Falls, I had much to draw from. The gifted program I directed there had an ongoing lecture series using medical, business, mental health, and college and university speakers. As an English teacher, I also used a wide variety of community resources in connection with complex themes in literature. They all educated me. The "Background" for many of the sessions in this book is based as much on that accumulation of information, ideas, materials, and thoughts as on formal coursework, training, and my private counseling practice, although the last three were certainly significant to this book.

contents

introduction   1

a note for parents   14

list of reproducible pages

introduction

about this book

description and benefits

Talk with Teens about Feelings, Family, Relationships, and the Future and its companion volume, *Talk with Teens about Self and Stress,* were written to meet the need of students to "just talk"—to share their feelings and concerns with supportive peers and an attentive adult. These guided discussions have evolved from many years of working with students, listening to them, and learning about their lives.

Since 1985, I have led short- and long-term groups ranging from grades 4 through 12, many of these groups for a full school term, for a total of over 1,400 sessions. I have also led single-session and short-term groups of adults. The suggestions, activities, and written exercises in this book, along with the flexible-focus format, have been thoroughly tested. You can feel confident about using these materials with your students and other group members.

I have witnessed the benefits of these guided discussion groups for students of many ages and ability levels.

- I have seen inspiring results in both well-adjusted teens and those at risk. Groups of students with high ability have also responded positively to this format.

- I have seen that "just talking" helps to lower stress levels, to normalize "weird" thoughts, and to sort out personal conflict.

- The groups give students who are cynical and negative an experience that makes school "not so bad."

- The groups help teens learn to anticipate problems and to find support for problem-solving.

- The groups serve a clearly preventive function in improving self-esteem and social ease. Participants feel better about themselves as they become comfortable with others and allow their "real selves" to show during group meetings. The interaction is affirming.

- Because the groups involve many students, teachers, counselors, and other group facilitators make good use of their own time in regard to student contact.

These are benefits that you will begin noticing and enjoying once your own group is established.

genesis

From 1962 through 1985, I taught junior and senior high school students in Iowa, Minnesota, South Dakota, and Berlin, Germany. My years in the classroom tuned me in to the social and emotional worlds of adolescents. When they responded to literature in their journals, when they interacted with me during yearbook meetings, when they worked with me in foreign-language club activities, and when they lingered after class, they told me about themselves.

I learned that they shared many common concerns, but with unique complexities. Most of my students wanted to "be known"—to be more than just another student, recognized for their individual worth and uniqueness. They readily accepted my invitation to respond personally, in journals, to the literature we were reading in class. I wanted them to learn to express themselves—on paper, in that case. We dialogued through notes in the margins. Such dialogue often replaced class discussion.

There were many reasons for this teaching approach. Some reasons relate to the groups I later developed. I wanted my students to become independent thinkers, to learn to trust that they had something worthwhile to say, and to discover what they thought and felt through expression. I also wanted to hear from *everyone*, not just from the highly verbal and assertive. The somewhat controlled format, with flexibility and open-endedness inherent, helped to accomplish all of those goals. The focus on individual expression would eventually become central to my discussion groups.

Some students stayed after class to ask advice, to talk about personal pain and growth, or, more frequently, to "just talk." Experiences like these are not uncommon in the teaching world. Students are hungry for acknowledgment and for nonjudgmental listening. I learned that there were many important things they did not discuss with their peers, and they did not always have a comfortable enough relationship with a parent to ask tough questions or express concern and anxiety.

My students, like those everywhere, were fatigued from part-time jobs and other responsibilities. They fought with siblings, broke up with sweethearts, and were scared of the future. Many struggled with the hypocrisy of the adults around them and the sad state of the world as they saw it; some were afraid to go home. Many responded to these and other issues with sadness and depression. They had a hard time balancing the fragments of their complex lives. Sometimes they felt like exploding from tension. They needed someone to talk to.

In 1985, when I became involved in gifted education, I thought back to the adolescents who had let me know them. I wondered if group discussions, held outside of the regular classroom, might help the high-stress students in the gifted program. I certainly had seen the need for support and attentive listening in the bright students who had been in my classes. I knew that, no matter what their level of capability, they were still adolescents, no more able than anyone else their age to deal with roller-coaster moods, galloping hormones, and conflicts with adults and peers. I decided to offer a group option to deal with social and emotional issues.

The group idea did not catch on immediately, but by the second semester there were three, with ten to twelve students each. The next year there were six groups, then ten, with two groups per day coordinated with the noon lunch schedule. Eventually adminis-

trators, counselors, student teachers, and guests from other districts came to watch, and almost invariably they would remark, "It's too bad *all* students can't have this opportunity." I agreed wholeheartedly. Observers also commented that they never would have suspected that students had so much to deal with behind their cool facades.

The students were faithful in attending the group meetings in spite of the fact that attendance was voluntary, though strongly encouraged. The groups became close through steady, undramatic weekly contact, and when there was a crisis, whether personal or institutional, there was a ready support system. The students taught me, they taught each other, and they learned about themselves. The topics were not necessarily "heavy," and the students responded to them, relaxing and "just talking."

I eventually wrote manuals for the groups and shared them. *Talk with Teens about Feelings, Family, Relationships, and the Future*, as well as *Talk with Teens about Self and Stress*, grew out of those manuals, their content tempered and shaped by years of experience.

purpose

The purpose of these guided discussion groups is to address the affective needs of adolescents. Through the groups, students gain self-awareness, and that in turn helps them to make better decisions, solve problems, and deal more effectively with their various environments. They learn to affirm themselves in all of their complexity, and they feel more in control of their lives.

It may be enough to say that the purpose of these groups is simply to let students express themselves—to "just talk." Adolescents need practice putting feelings and concerns into words. As much as some of them talk socially, they nevertheless may not be skilled at communicating their feelings honestly and with clarity. Later in life, their relationships and their employment will be enhanced if they are able to talk about what is important to them. Adolescence is a good time to learn those skills. Discussion groups can provide an arena for learning and practicing them.

- A group can provide a noncompetitive environment where no grades are given and where everyone is fairly equal.

- In the affective realm, students have much in common. Everyone is navigating the uneven seas of adolescence, with complex feelings,

2

frustrations, and anxieties, and without the skills to ensure smooth sailing. Discussion groups can provide a place for safe talk about this journey.

According to the feedback students have given me for many years, the topics covered here often are not discussed, even among best friends. In end-of-the-year written assessments, students have told me that they are grateful for having received guidance in important areas of their lives—and for having been "forced" to deal with these topics in a safe, supportive environment.

Students inevitably gain social skills through group interaction. Often, social discomfort contributes to, and is exacerbated by, poor functioning in school. Learning about what they and others have in common, learning to listen, gaining experience in initiating and responding socially, and becoming aware of how they are seen by others all work to promote social ease and enhance self-esteem, both of which can help to make school a more pleasant place.

The format of this book is not designed specifically and formally to teach group skills or to acquaint students with the vocabulary of group process. However, many such skills and some helpful terminology will likely be learned along the way. Guided group discussion is a process-more-than-product activity, yet one goal is certainly to enhance the skill of articulating social and emotional concerns. The focus, the objectives, and the suggestions for content and closure contained in each session should provide enough of a framework that group members will have good, solid, invigorating experiences.

It is important to understand that the purpose of these groups is not to "fix" students. Even though the questions are designed to provoke a healthy level of introspection, the emphasis is always on the experience of articulating feelings and thoughts in the presence of others who listen and care. These are not meant to be therapy groups. Of course, some noticeable changes in attitude and behavior may occur, but even when it may appear that these are brought about by the response and support of the group, other factors, such as changes at home, the healing effect of time, or developmental leaps, may also have contributed. A group might simply help to *sustain* a student through a difficult year.

As is the case whenever adults stand firmly beside adolescents for a time, establish trust, and participate in their complex lives, you will serve your students best by hearing them well and offering support as they find their own direction.

assumptions

The format and content of this book reflect the following assumptions, which you may want to keep in mind as you lead your own group.

1. All adolescents have a desire to be heard, listened to, taken seriously, and respected.

2. Some adolescents who are quiet, shy, intimidated, or untrusting will not spontaneously offer comments, but they, too, want to be recognized and understood as unique individuals.

3. All adolescents need support, no matter how strong and successful they seem.

4. All adolescents feel stressed at times. Some feel stressed most or even all of the time.

5. All adolescents are sensitive to family tension. Some are trying hard to keep their families afloat or intact. They may be unaware of it, but they might even be using bad behavior to keep their parents focused on them—and together.

6. All adolescents feel angry at times.

7. All adolescents feel socially inept and uncomfortable at times.

8. All adolescents worry about the future at times.

9. All adolescents, no matter how smooth and self-confident they may appear, need practice talking honestly about feelings.

10. Everyone wears a facade at times.

about the sessions

general description

The guided discussion sessions in *Talk with Teens about Feelings, Family, Relationships, and the Future* are appropriate for these populations:

- the general population

- a number of special populations

- any adolescent age level, with possible adjustments in vocabulary, session length, and content for younger groups and for some ability levels.

The vocabulary used in explanatory material is appropriate for teachers and counselors. In the written exercises, it is geared up rather than down, since it is generally easier to make adjustments for younger children than in the other direction. Older adolescents, especially those with high ability, respond better to language that challenges rather than patronizes.

For some junior high/middle school groups, some written exercises may need to be shortened and some vocabulary changed. Some of the suggestions might not fit, depending on the setting and the group's intellectual level. Some of the sessions assume a high abstract-reasoning ability, and some deal with issues that are suitable only for mature students. You will need to assess the individual sessions to determine which ones might be most helpful, enjoyable, and appropriate for your group. Be sure not to underestimate your students' awareness of the world just because they are chronologically young. At the same time, you will need to consider developmental realities and community sensitivities.

Special populations who might benefit from these guided group discussions include these:

- students at risk for dropping out
- students with behavior problems
- students who are shy or lonely
- students having difficulty with adult authority
- teenage parents
- underachievers
- students with high ability who may have been labeled "gifted"
- students in, or returning from, treatment for substance abuse or eating disorders
- students in transition during family changes, including death, divorce, and remarriage.

Sessions are arranged in a purposeful progression, but may be rearranged to create a short-term program or to accommodate part of a particular agenda.

focus

Why have a focus for each session? All students are not as flexible as they might seem, even if they appear to be quite "unstructured." On the other hand, some are quite flexible, and, especially if they are verbal and spontaneous, they may prefer a loose format. They might say, "Just let us come in here and hang out. We'll find something to talk about." However,

many are in the other camp, and they quickly tire of "not really doing anything."

Students who are more orderly and structured like to know that time spent in a group is worthwhile in more specific terms than just "feeling good." Lacking a focus, if the group is a voluntary activity, they will choose not to come when something else is more inviting or pressing. They might also object to the fact that assertive members set the pace and topic each time. Students with new and dramatic needs each week can quickly dominate, and others will either defer and listen—or leave, frustrated that their own issues are not being addressed. Discussion groups should not be just for natural talkers and crises. Everyday matters are also worth discussing.

On the other hand, group discussions need not be rigidly programmed. Although this book proposes a focus for each session, with several sessions building on a theme, there is great potential for nimbly changing direction during discussion. A good leader can accommodate various strands that need to be pursued, yet still gently steer the group to closure, overtly acknowledging that the focus inspired unexpected directions. Especially with topics students may perceive as intimidating and difficult, the focus is an excuse to persist with tough questions and deal with issues and problems, not just gripes and frustrations.

In addition, having a focus makes it easy for you to communicate with administrators, parents, and other faculty about your group and what you do together. Many outsiders assume that discussion groups are for teacher-bashing, for airing family secrets, for shaping up disruptive students, or for rewarding good students, as if the meetings were some kind of elitist "dessert." Being able to say, "We've been dealing with relationships for the past four weeks," or "We're focusing on planning for the future this semester," or, more specifically, "We've been talking about dealing with anger and other strong emotions," helps to lessen any such anxiety and also underscores that your group is dealing with substance.

objectives and suggestions

The objectives listed for each session tell you what to work toward and what to expect if the general suggestions are followed. They are not meant to be read to the students. They also may be useful in communicating content to administrators, parents, and teachers who wonder what your group is doing. You may want to prepare a list of objectives for parent conferences, for example.

The suggestions are just that—suggestions. Use all, some, or none of them, and adapt those you use to meet the needs of your group. Time limits and group temperament are two of many factors you will want to consider when choosing which suggestions and activities to pursue.

activity sheets

Several of the sessions include activity sheets that may be photocopied for group use. In my experience, these written exercises do not make discussions too structured, and most students do not resist them. It all depends on how they are used.

Especially when they are not used too often, students actually *appreciate* the handouts for giving them an opportunity to think quietly and focus at the outset of a meeting; to write, objectify, and perhaps edit their thoughts; and to sort and ponder complex issues. Everyone has a chance to be heard. Shy members can share without having to compete with assertive folks. Discussion can involve only a few or all of the questions or items, and the students can be polled for categories of responses or asked for specific answers.

Many of the sessions in this book deal with topics where confidentiality might be a concern. Therefore, for sessions that use activity sheets, I usually recommend that you collect and dispose of them at the end of the session. You might also direct group members to tear up their own handouts and leave them in a container in the meeting room. This will not only help to protect privacy, but will underscore that the activity sheets are filled out to aid discussion, not to become part of anyone's file—sometimes a concern for both students and parents.

As an alternative, you may want to keep file folders for all group members and have them leave their activity sheets in their folders at the close of each session. This will ensure that sensitive handouts don't end up on the classroom floor or circulating through the halls, with personal thoughts revealed indiscreetly through carelessness. Tell group members that they can decide what to do with their activity sheets when the group experience comes to an end. They might choose to return to some of the activity sheets later in

a series of sessions, checking on where they have been and commenting on how circumstances have changed.

background information

For many of the sessions, a few paragraphs of background information are provided at the beginning. Like the objectives, the background is not meant to be read to the students. It is designed to help you prepare for the session and think broadly about the topic at hand; to offer some basic information about the topic that might be useful to you during the session; to inspire further reading; to encourage you to anticipate student concerns; and to assist you in determining a possible direction for the discussion, according to the needs of your group.

This work is a synthesis of several years' worth of information gleaned from seminars, workshops, in-service training, lectures, course work, consultation with experts, and my own experience interacting with adolescents in my teaching and counseling careers. The background contains some of what I have accumulated.

closure

Each session includes a suggestion for closure. It is always a good idea to end a session with some kind of summary or tying-up activity, whether you provide it yourself or offer your students the opportunity. Inherent in closure is the reminder that their discussions are purposeful, that they share common concerns, and that they have been heard. Making a habit of systematic closure sends a message that time will be provided and protected for pulling strands together and reflecting. Group members will learn that bringing up new topics is not appropriate for those final moments. If a new strand does appear, suggest that it be held for discussion at the next session—and check then to see if it is still a concern.

sessions for special populations

- Groups geared to family transitions can especially benefit from all or most of the sessions in the Focus: Feelings section.
- Students at risk, with behavior problems, or dealing with substance abuse might be helped by sessions such as these:

- ▶ In Focus: Feelings: "Mood Range," "Unfair," "Disappointment," "Anger," and "Sadness and Depression"
- ▶ In Focus: Family: "Personal Space and Privacy" and "Becoming Separate"
- ▶ In Focus: Relationships: "Friendship," "Conformity," "With Parents," "With Siblings," and "With Teachers"
- ▶ In Focus: The Future: "Open to Change," "What Is Maturity?" "Finding Meaning," and "Anxiety."

■ Groups focusing on depression often find many of the sessions in Focus: Feelings and Focus: Relationships to be helpful. "Family Roles" and "Personal Space and Privacy" in Focus: Family might also be pertinent.

■ *All* sessions are appropriate for groups geared to the social and emotional needs of individuals with high ability. Be aware that many students at risk have high ability. Also be aware that students with high ability may have high stress levels, may be significantly distressed by their families, relationships, and environments, and may, in fact, be particularly at risk for depression, eating disorders, and other stress-related maladies. Like other adolescents, they need to gain skills in articulating personal concerns and to find support among their peers.

forming a group
group size

In my experience, ideal group size varies according to age level. For students of high school age, between eight and twelve is optimal. With more than twelve, it is difficult to hear from everyone adequately on any subject, especially when using an activity sheet. With fewer than eight, there is less opportunity for variety in input, and there is a possibility that familiarity will interfere with seriousness of purpose.

For students of junior high/middle school age, a group size of six to eight seems to work best. Class periods in the school setting are shorter, and students need more time and individual attention to articulate their thoughts and attain depth.

group composition

I have found that the best groups are often those where members do not know each other well outside the group. They seem to feel more free to share, and they do not have to preface all comments with "Well, someone in here has heard me say this before, but...." On the other hand, I have also had good groups where most members knew each other well. They became even better acquainted through the group sessions.

Depending on the size of the population you will draw from, you may not have a choice. If the members of your group know each other, it is important to move the group beyond the natural division of "friends" and "non-friends." Having a focus, with specific activities and written exercises, helps to ensure that the "friends" group does not dominate or antagonize the others with inside humor. Encouraging them to change seating each time can also be helpful.

I like to promote the idea of using the groups to break down barriers. For general discussion groups, I prefer to mix achievers and underachievers, at-risk and not at-risk, highly involved and not-so-involved. Otherwise, each continues to stereotype the other, with the "in" or successful students feeling no common ground with the disenfranchised or low-achieving students, and vice versa. The affective emphasis helps them all to connect with each other non-hierarchically and with shared humanness.

If several groups are being formed at one time, I recommend that you initially compile a list of all students who accept the invitation to participate and then sort the list. Of course, recruitment will have to target those not likely to feel welcome. In some cases, the highest-functioning students may be the most reluctant to join, fearing that the groups are geared only to problems and that participation will somehow stigmatize them. Students at risk and underachieving students may think that they are the only ones with stresses, vulnerabilities, and fears. All group members have a great deal to learn from each other, and the group setting can be an ideal learning environment.

Students with high ability are often not comfortable talking about social and emotional concerns in intellectually heterogeneous groups. Many of their problems and concerns are similar to those of other students, but usually they share more easily when others of similar intellect are there to hear them and can express concerns at a similar level. Perhaps it is also easier to let down the facade—and not protect "image"—with those they feel can empathize with them. A mixture of various levels of *achievement*, not *ability*, can make highly productive discussion groups for students with high capability. Often, under-achievers are amazed that achievers have social and emotional problems; some achievers are equally amazed that underachievers can be highly intelligent. Provoking that discovery of common ground is a good place to start.

If mixing is not possible in your setting, or if your group is homogeneous regarding an area of concern and has a specific purpose and agenda, you can still use these guided discussions with confidence, since they deal with common adolescent issues.

Mixing genders is also good, even though it is not always possible and might not be advantageous or appropriate for certain topics. However, it is important for males and females to learn about each other in a safe and honest environment, outside of the regular classroom and apart from usual social settings. It is also important for students of both genders to learn how to communicate with, and in the presence of, each other.

Especially for students who are shy or who have little social experience, a discussion group can provide a chance to have contact with the other gender. But even for the highly social, a group can raise awareness of gender issues and enhance males' and females' ability to function effectively with each other in social relationships now and in the future, in employment, and perhaps even in the board room someday.

On the other hand, same-gender grouping also has advantages and is particularly appropriate when the issues are gender-specific, especially troublesome and gender-related, or perceived to be unsafe for discussion with members of the other gender. The age of group members might be a determining factor in regard to the last aspect. Same-gender groups can sometimes empower students in ways that mixed groups cannot. Homogeneity may be especially desirable in a first-stage recovery group, for example, or when a topic may be related to trauma. Obviously, decisions about grouping must also be based on the goals and purpose of a group.

Because the sessions are mostly geared to social and emotional concerns, not to intellectual or academic concerns, it is best to try for homogeneity regarding age. High school juniors and seniors are a lot alike, but most seniors are looking ahead more intensely. Sophomore issues are usually different from

junior issues, and even seventh and eighth graders often have a difficult time connecting with each other about social and emotional concerns. Relationship and separation issues also differ along the age continuum, and it is best when students can communicate with others in their own age group.

Granted, boys and girls may differ greatly in physical and emotional maturity, particularly in junior high/middle school. Still, a less mature boy can gain from hearing about the concerns of the girls he is around daily, and probably vice versa.

getting students to join

The best way to get students to join your group, especially in a school setting, is to invite them personally. In any event, I recommend that you *not* call it a "counseling group" when describing it to prospective group members. Some students are automatically turned off and turned away by that label. Later on, should someone ask if, in fact, it is a counseling group, you might explain that "counseling" basically means "talking and listening" with someone trained in the process, and, in that regard, your group might be called a counseling group. However, for recruitment purposes, "discussion group" is both accurate and more appealing. It carries no negative stigma.

"Support group" is appropriate when there is a common, specific agenda or a shared problem area. If the group is largely preventive, with self-awareness and personal growth as goals, then "support" can sound too problem-oriented for many students. In any case, "discussion group" is my preference.

I have contacted students individually to explain a proposed group, and I have called in small groups and full-size discussion groups to hear the plan. In either situation, you will want to assure the students that joining the group is not a dangerous thing to do. The advantage of calling in the group as a whole is that the students can see who else will be attending. On the other hand, some might decide against joining for that very reason, without giving the group a chance. When meeting with students individually, it is good to give them the names of a few prospective members—if they ask, and if it is appropriate to share names in advance.

Be sure to emphasize the social as well as the emotional purposes of the group. Students respond well to the idea of getting to know new people and learning to know current acquaintances and friends in new ways. They also can relate to the idea of talking about adolescent stress. Explain that, beyond pursuing general goals, the group will help to determine its own unique direction. That much of an explanation usually suffices. If students want to know more, show them the table of contents for this book. The session titles are varied, and students usually find them interesting, pertinent, and unexpected.

Especially for high school students, it helps to tell them that once you get to know them better through the group experience, you will be able to write more complete and accurate job, college, or scholarship recommendations for them when they are needed. Explain that you will also be a better and more informed advocate for them if they ever need assistance.

how to approach students at risk

If your group is to serve students at risk in a school setting, there will probably be school or district guidelines for identifying prospective group members. Identifying factors might include the following. Students with any level of ability may be found in each of these categories:

- family disruption
- substance abuse
- physical or sexual abuse
- family tragedy
- significant underachievement
- lack of family support for school attendance or achievement
- a potential for dropping out of school.

Some teens at risk might be eager to join a group, but many probably will not be. If attendance is voluntary, meet with prospective members individually and privately. Explain that you will be leading a discussion group for those who are dealing with stress, and you are inviting them to participate. If the student is a rebel, someone who is anti-authority, an underachiever with high ability, or a "joker," state that you are looking for interesting, complex persons who can help to make a good group. Say that you are looking specifically for individuals who express their abilities in unusual ways. Explain that you don't want a group that is afraid to challenge and think or that always does what is expected and predictable. Reframing characteristics that are usually considered

troublesome in this way often takes students by surprise and encourages them to participate.

However, no matter what a particular person's behavior might be, always present the group's purpose honestly: to give members a chance to "just talk" about issues that are important to all adolescents. Be sincere, accepting, and supportive in your invitation. With students at risk, as with all prospective group members, take care not to frighten them away by sounding too invasive or personal. Give them time to warm up to the idea of interacting with others about personal issues.

assessing your readiness to lead discussion groups

If you are not used to dealing with groups in an informal discussion setting, you may find it helpful to keep the following suggestions and observations in mind:

- For most adolescents, the affective dimension involves more personal risk-taking than the academic. Social and emotional areas are much less "controllable" than the intellectual realm.

- Significant people in their lives might have focused more on academic than on affective needs. Some individuals will be eager and immediately grateful for the emphasis on the social and emotional; some might be uncomfortable or skeptical at first; some might even be frightened by it. Whatever the response, your concentrated attention on the affective will probably be a new experience for them.

- If you are careful to stick to social and emotional issues, there will be little opportunity for students to play competitive, one-up verbal games, especially since these issues are less likely to be debatable.

- Recognize that some group members may be more intellectually nimble than you are. On the other hand, some may be less nimble, and you will need to be patient. In the social and emotional realm, usually no one feels like an expert, including the group leader. Tell that to your group.

You might also want to consider your motives for establishing groups, as well as your sense of security around various types of adolescents. Ask yourself these questions:

- "Can I avoid feeling competitive with them, or needing to assert control over them?"

- "Can I not be threatened by them?" (Remember, you have longer life experience.)

- "Can I stay focused on their social and emotional issues?"

- "Can I deal with them simply as human beings with frailties, insecurities, sensitivities, and vulnerabilities, regardless of their achievements or lack of achievement?"

- "Can I avoid needing to put them in their place?"

- "Can I accept their defenses, such as arrogance or rebelliousness, at the outset, and give them time to let themselves be vulnerable?"

- "Can I recognize that they may not be accomplished risk-takers socially, academically, and/or emotionally, and that they might need to be encouraged to take appropriate risks?"

- "Can I look honestly at some of my own stereotypes or negative feelings that might interfere in my work with various populations, and can I put them aside for the duration of the group experience?"

- "Can I resist voyeurism, needing to be 'in the know' about their personal lives, and gossiping about them?"

- "Can I let them teach me about themselves, instead of my needing to teach them?"

If you can answer "yes" to all or most of these questions, don't worry—you're ready to take on a roomful of students. If you aren't feeling quite ready but want to learn how to be an effective discussion group leader, find someone who has experience in this area and is willing to serve as a mentor for you, perhaps by agreeing to co-facilitate a group.

guidelines for group leaders
general guidelines

The following general guidelines are designed to help you lead successful and meaningful discussion groups. You may want to review them from time to time over the life of a group:

1. Be prepared to learn how to lead a group by *doing* it. Let the students know that this is your attitude. If you are in a school setting and you are not a trained counselor, ask a school counselor for information on group process and counseling techniques. As noted above, you might also arrange to co-facilitate your first group with a counselor or trained group leader. Even if you lead groups regularly, an occasional refresher on group process is a good idea.

2. Don't think that you have to be an expert on every topic covered. Tell the students at the outset that you want to learn *with them* and *from them.* That is a wonderful place to start, and your students will respond. For most sessions, having all of the right information is not the key to success. Trust your adult wisdom; it will serve you well. That's one thing you have that your students don't.

3. Monitor group interaction and work toward contribution from everyone without making that an issue. Remember that shy students can gain a great deal just by listening. Of course, you will want to encourage everyone to participate, but never insist. The activity sheets can be used to provide quiet students with a comfortable opening for sharing.

4. Keep the session focus in mind, but be flexible about direction. Your group may lead you in new directions that are as worthwhile as the stated focus and suggestions.

5. It is probably best to go into each session with two sessions in mind, since the one you have planned may not get as much response as expected. You can always unobtrusively guide the group in a new direction. Try several approaches to a topic before dropping it, however. It might simply require some "baking time."

6. Be *willing* to role model everything, even though it may not usually be necessary for promoting group interaction. (See page 16, tip #9, for cautionary statements in this regard.) We all benefit from positive role models, and if you aren't willing to self-disclose, group members may wonder why they should be expected to reveal their thoughts and feelings.

7. Every now and then, check out how the students are feeling about the group process. Is there anything they would like to do differently or change? Are they comfortable sharing their feelings and concerns? What has been helpful? Have they noticed any problems that need addressing? (Be prepared for comments related to their perception that discussions are being dominated by a few, there is not enough flexibility in direction, a personality conflict causes tension within the group, or there is too much leader direction.) This processing provides an opportunity for students to practice tact in addressing group issues. Ask for suggestions and incorporate those that fit the overall purpose of the group. Be aware that some students may press for "no focus" for a long time. You may want to review the rationale for having a focus as outlined on page 4. Depending on the makeup of your group, you may choose to delay questions about format until the benefits have become fairly clear. Or simply be prepared to explain the purpose of the format while emphasizing that the format is flexible. Support the group and give guidance as they make progress in overcoming group problems.

8. If group energy consistently or increasingly lags, discuss that in group. Let the students help you figure out how to energize the discussions and/or deal with group inhibitions. However, do not readily reject the idea of maintaining a focus for each session. Perhaps you need to check out your questioning style, or more deftly follow some strands that come up spontaneously. Or perhaps you need to be more selective in choosing your topics. The activity sheets can help to encourage sharing. My recommendation is that group members *write* their responses, in order to encourage more than just vague thinking.

open-ended vs. closed questions

In general, open-ended questions are best for generating discussion and should be used most of the time. "Why might someone...," "How would you describe...," and "What are some examples..." insist on more than "yes" or "no" responses, and are likely to elicit information that will encouraged responses from others.

Closed, yes/no questions also have their place, but they should be used judiciously. Most adolescents do not eagerly elaborate, especially when a group is newly formed, and a "yes" or a nod from a hesitant individual can be a low-risk step toward sharing more information later. The next question, however, might then be an open-ended one to the whole group: "What do the rest of you think about that? What experiences have you had?" In addition, asking a closed question to the entire group, and slowly getting nods from several group members, can give the group a chance to think about an idea for a few seconds before being asked for examples or personal experiences. In fact, a second closed question to the group can offer even more time for thought before asking for examples. Be aware that examples do not always come to mind readily, and group members may need several seconds to decide if it is safe to share a personal experience. In the meantime, calmly wait with an expectant posture and facial expression.

Closed questions may also be appropriate during closure. Affirmative nods in response to a "Was the session thought-provoking?" can provide positive closure, especially when little or no time remains. Obviously, open-ended questions like "What was particularly helpful?" are appropriate when there is enough time remaining to hear from several group members.

ethical behavior

Your ethical behavior as group leader has great importance. Sharing confidential group information in the teachers' lounge, with parents, or in the community will not only be hurtful, but may also ultimately destroy the possibility of any group activity in your school. Trust is quickly lost, and it is difficult or even impossible to reestablish.

If you are a teacher and plan to conduct groups in a school setting, but are unfamiliar with ethical guidelines for counselors, get a copy of such guidelines from your school counselor and read them thoroughly.

Be especially aware of your responsibilities regarding confidentiality. This includes familiarizing yourself with situations in which confidentiality may be waived, such as when abuse is suspected, when someone is in danger or may be a danger to others, or when there is a court order. The "informed consent" aspect can be addressed by discussing format, content, confidentiality, and purpose when extending the invitation to attend the group, or at the first meeting.

You may wish to address these issues in a letter to parents, asking their permission for their children to attend the group. For a sample letter (which you may modify to include these issues), see page 18. Please note that this letter is intended for groups not designed for specific problem areas. Feel free to adapt it accordingly.

journal-writing

Depending on the purpose of your group, whether it is mandatory or voluntary, what other responsibilities group members have, and the level of access group members will have to you outside of group meetings, you might consider inviting them to do some journal-writing. Keep the following points in mind as you extend the invitation:

- Groups that serve special populations, and are consciously therapeutic, can benefit greatly from journal-writing and leader feedback.

- Journal-writing can add a valuable dimension to any group experience. Having an opportunity to put thoughts into writing often helps participants to articulate, clarify, expand on, and sort ideas and issues that are important to them. They are more likely to remember ideas and issues they want to bring up in the group, and they feel more confident about expressing them.

- An important goal of the group experience is learning to articulate thoughts and feelings in order to enhance relationships with friends, parents, and boyfriends/girlfriends now, and with co-workers, college roommates, spouses/partners, and children in the future. Journal-writing—with encouragement from you to share in the group some of the gist or specifics of what they write—can aid in this learning process. Some group members who are not assertive may express themselves more comfortably on paper.

- Some adolescents eagerly write their feelings, a fact that is obvious in the sometimes voluminous notes that are passed in junior and senior high schools. Others see writing as a burdensome chore. Sometimes this reflects a negative experience with writing in the classroom. Reassure the group that their journal-writing will not be graded. They will not have to worry about punctuation, spelling, sentence structure, or any of the other mechanics of writing. What is important is what they have to say, not how they choose to say it.

- Some individuals have a strong aversion to writing, perhaps because they prefer another mode of creative expression. Visual artists, musicians, and kinesthetic learners sometimes find it difficult to write—or to sustain writing. You might encourage those students to use their journals as "sketchbooks" or as "idea scrapbooks." They may draw or doodle, include poems or scripts, create cartoons with captions—anything they choose, as long as their efforts communicate their feelings.

- In schools where there is considerable journal-writing in language arts classes, students are less likely to welcome journals in the discussion groups. There can definitely be "journal burnout." Be sensitive to this issue while explaining that journal-writing during the group experience will probably be very different from journal-writing in their regular classes. Rather than writing about specific topics, they will have the chance to explore their feelings and issues that matter to them.

- Students often need strong enticement to join groups, especially when groups are first being established. They are most receptive when the group experience does not seem like "work." Journal-writing can easily be perceived as an "assignment" or "work"—"more of the same"—and turn students off. Explain that it is always simply an option if, in fact, it is not mandatory. Sell it as an opportunity, rather than as an assignment. Encourage reluctant writers to give it a try.

- Invite all journal-writers to share their journals with you. This can give them a chance to communicate privately with you about important concerns that cannot be comfortably discussed in the group. You then can respond by writing in the margins. This is a good way to carry on a dialogue with those who may not feel comfortable sharing their thoughts and feelings orally within the group. It gives everyone a chance for one-on-one communication with the group leader, and conscientious feedback is appreciated and essential. However, journals should not take the place of "just talking." Remind reluctant talkers that while you look forward to reading their journals, and you appreciate their sharing them with you, you hope they will also contribute to the group discussion.

dealing with group members who are quiet or shy

Earnest efforts to ask students who are quiet or shy for at least one or two comments each meeting can help them to feel included and gradually increase their courage or willingness to share. Although listening can be as valuable as speaking in finding commonalities and gaining self-awareness, it is important for reticent students to be heard by their peers, if only at modest levels. Even "small talk" between a leader and a shy student while everyone is getting settled contributes to comfort and ease, which eventually might help to generate spontaneous comments.

The value of communication with peers, in contrast to communication with the leader, should not be underestimated. Post-group feedback has indicated that quiet students gain as much or more than assertive students from the group experience. The fact that the dominant American culture values extroversion and assertiveness often makes natural reticence seem odd. Groups can actually help to affirm quiet personal styles. Perhaps a lack of sharing with peers prior to, and outside of, the group experience has left quiet students feeling poorly informed and "on the outside." Just listening to other group members can be valuable. Using the activity sheets gives everyone, including shy students, a chance to receive the attention of the group and be heard.

counseling individual group members

I have found that when a level of trust has been established in the group and between students and leader, individuals with pressing needs will seek out the leader outside of the group. That assumes, of course, that the leader is accessible.

If you will not be on the premises every day, it is important to make an announcement in the group about times when you are available. If you have created an atmosphere that is safe for communication, your group members will likely trust you to be there in times of crisis or for special concerns. However, as in everything, moderation is the key. Too much emphasis at group sessions on outside conferencing can turn off students who do not want to connect the groups to counseling.

handling emotional bombshells

Most adolescents are appropriately discreet in what they share in group, especially when the leader does not pry or *need* to know private information. However, you can probably expect a few highly charged moments to occur along the way, most often because someone suddenly shares what may be an "emotional bombshell."

What happens when something shocking comes out, when someone breaks down and cries, or when intense conflict arises within the group? No one can predict these events with any accuracy, of course, since every group has its own unique dynamics, and groups, by nature, are full of surprises. However, you can learn to trust your instincts. With time and experience, you will be able to anticipate and deal with crisis situations and even avert them, depending on the purpose of your group.

If they occur, you can be prepared. Have tissues handy for someone who cries, but affirm the emotion in your facial expression and body language and accept the tears as real and valid. When appropriate, ask the student what, if anything, he or she would like from the group. Verbal or nonverbal support? A hug? Or is it best for the group just to listen?

If a student makes a dramatic revelation, immediately remind the group about the importance of confidentiality. You might say, quietly, "It probably took courage for (name of student) to share that. It wasn't easy. She/he trusted you as a group. Remember—what comes out in the group stays in the group. If you are tempted to share this with someone outside the group, bite your tongue. That's very important. We want to protect our group." Beware of exaggerated responses, both nonverbal and verbal, which can reinforce the idea that a particular revelation is "too much to handle." In fact, the sharer might have been testing that belief. Some group members may have high anxiety about emotions and honest sharing, as a result of environment and experience.

If yours is a school group, and you are not a trained counselor, you may need to consult with a school counselor or administrator to learn what to do in specific situations. For example, if someone drops an emotional bombshell about abuse or suicide, you will want to know about mandatory reporting and how to follow up. Your district likely has guidelines specific to these issues. It is best to know them ahead of time. The same guidelines hold true for working with community youth groups.

Groups are ideal settings for practicing conflict resolution. Help those in disagreement to talk it out. If yours is a school group, and you are not a counselor, pursue helpful material on conflict resolution in your school library, or ask your school counselor for strategies to deal with dissension. Be aware of your own possible resistance to dealing with conflict. Your own fears might prevent your students from handling the situation in a healthy manner.

keeping the topic a secret

If your group is voluntary and a session topic is announced in advance, some students may elect not to come if the topic doesn't immediately sound interesting or personally applicable to them. You will want group attendance to be consistent; it is distracting and damaging when ten students show up one week and only two the next. Therefore, I recommend that you use a "trust me" response when students ask about the next session's topic. Suggest that they show up and be surprised. Remind them that one can never anticipate the interesting directions a particular topic might take. Besides, many topics are more complex than they first appear.

other uses for these guided group discussions

in the regular classroom

Talk with Teens about Feelings, Family, Relationships, and the Future can also be useful in the regular classroom. Weekly discussions, or a limited daily series of units, can be part of the curriculum in health, home economics, life skills, social science, or language arts, among several possibilities. Discussion is particularly meaningful for students when it deals with the self. Class periods spent in home room, or "community," when designed to enhance self-esteem and create positive interaction in a school, can use these sessions effectively if the time allowed is adequate.

Group dynamics differ, of course, depending on whether a particular class has thirty students or ten, but the focus and most of the strategies work with both. Since a discussion of an activity sheet can easily take an hour with a group of ten, adjustments must be made when activity sheets are used with larger groups. Classes can be divided into small groups for sharing, for example. In general, expect less intimacy and spontaneity in a full classroom, but don't underestimate the value of focused discussion in a large group.

to promote cohesion in school and other groups

Selected sessions can be adapted for use in promoting group cohesion and in raising awareness of self and others in athletic and academic teams, in music groups, and in school clubs. They may also serve the same purpose in church and community groups, governors' schools, special summer programs for adolescents, women's or men's conferences and retreats, and staff development sessions. "Mood Range," "Happiness," "Being Interesting," and "What Is Maturity?" are examples of sessions that might be adapted for these purposes. The companion to this book, *Talk with Teens about Self and Stress*, includes several sessions particularly appropriate for group-building and raising awareness.

a note for parents

Talk with Teens about Feelings, Family, Relationships, and the Future can be a valuable tool for getting to know your adolescents. It can help you to access what they are thinking and feeling, the issues that are important to them, their problems, and their hopes and plans for the future.

You may have noticed that parents and teenagers often have difficulty sustaining conversations (yes, probably an understatement). Sometimes it's hard to know what to talk about besides school work and headphones. Parents often don't know what subjects are safe and what subjects are taboo. Sometimes *all* subjects seem to be off limits.

Students may say to someone outside the family, "There are just some things I'm not comfortable telling my parents—or asking them." Teenage sons and daughters tend to be moody, becoming more and more quiet and private at home. This book can give you a way to break down some barriers that have gone up since your children entered the teenage years.

Scan the "Background" and "Suggestions" in each session for possible topics and conversation-starters. These sections will also provide you with insights into developmental issues that both you and your children may be wrestling with. Parents often forget what adolescence felt like, and the information in the sessions can help to remind you of the complexities involved. In general, when talking to your teen, "Teach me about what it means to be your age" often gets better results than a parent-dominated, presentation-of-information approach.

Most of the sessions in this book—especially those in the sections titled Focus: Feelings and Focus: Family—can serve as catalysts for family discussion. In groups I have led over the years, many teens have taken the activity sheets home for their parents to fill out. Many personal issues remain with us as adults and are good to discuss even with young adolescents, who are beginning to be aware that these are their issues, too. Questions posed can provoke important self-disclosure in us as parents. Such sharing can be helpful to adolescents in pursuit of their own identity. We are never "done" with many issues in our lives, and it is good to admit our humanness to our growing children. Such non-authoritarian "realness" can help to create dialogue and can also lessen the feelings in adolescents of being judged and being strange.

getting started

how to begin

Begin the first meeting by letting the students know how pleased and excited you are that they will be part of the group. Remind them that the purpose of the group is to "just talk"—to share their feelings and concerns with each other and with you, and to offer and accept support.

Be sure to explain that, during group meetings, you will not be a "teacher" in the usual sense of the word. Instead, the focus will be on them. You will be their guide, listening carefully and sharing your own insights when appropriate, but mostly helping them to connect with each other. Emphasize that you will all learn from each other.

Move next to introductions and a get-acquainted activity, such as "An Introductory Exercise" on page 20. Tell the students to read through all of the sentence beginnings silently and slowly and complete each thought in writing. Then invite them to "read down" their sentences. Or, if you prefer, go directly to the session you have chosen to start the group.

At some point during your first meeting, distribute copies of the "Group Guidelines" on page 19. Go over them one at a time, using a tone of voice that suggests they are positive, not heavy-handed. Read them aloud or ask for volunteers to read them. Ask if anyone has questions, or if there is anything they don't understand. Tell the students that everyone is expected to follow these guidelines for as long as the group exists—including you. Explain that although they may not know how to do all of these things and behave in all of these ways right now, they will be learning and practicing these skills over the life of the group.

how to proceed

First-year groups, particularly at younger ages, often need more structure than more experienced groups. It also takes a while to establish ease and fluidity in discussion, especially when group members are not acquainted outside of the group. At experienced levels, students are able to deal with more abstract and personal topics with little introduction, and they are likely to be more patient and tolerant about experimenting with format. First-year groups of older teens usually attain depth more quickly than younger groups, although the presence of even one or two spontaneous, honest middle schoolers can move a young group quickly into significant interaction.

Follow the suggestions for introducing each topic, for generating discussion, and for managing the written activities. You will probably find many more suggestions than you will need for a session. Teachers and counselors who used my original manuals told me that they appreciated having several suggestions from which to choose, and that is why I have included many here.

You may find it difficult to follow the printed text while leading the discussions. Rather than reading anything word-for-word to your group, it is best to familiarize yourself thoroughly with the content of a session before meeting with the students. Then you will have in mind a general direction and some ideas for pursuing various discussion strands, while keeping an eye on the session materials.

Sometimes your group may generate a good discussion for the entire session from only the first suggestion. This is to be expected, and there is nothing wrong with that. Never feel that you need to finish everything I have suggested. Be flexible.

Be aware that even when students enjoy the group, they can forget to come to meetings. If your group is voluntary, you may need to remind the students for several weeks about meeting times and places. Eventually attendance will become a habit.

tips for group leaders

1. Remind participants that anything said in the group stays in the group. Confidentiality is especially important when sensitive information is shared.

2. Ask open-ended questions, not "yes" and "no" questions, to generate discussion. "How...," "What...," "Why...," and "Could..." are preferable to "Is...," "Are...," and "Did..." for asking questions. However, be aware that closed yes/no questions can be used effectively to check out consensus in the group, to provoke thought before asking follow-up questions, and during closure. In addition, for reluctant students, closed questions such as "Was it a sad time?" offer low risk.

3. Respond with "Tell us more about...," "Put words on that feeling...," "Help us understand...," "Can you give an example of...," or "What do you mean by...."

4. Always allow group members to "pass" if they prefer not to speak. This applies to any group activity, including discussions and activity sheets. Make it clear from the beginning that nobody ever *has* to speak, even though you hope you can get to know *all* of them through the discussions.

5. Don't preach, and don't moralize. They probably hear enough of that elsewhere. This experience should be different. Too many "shoulds" can shut down spontaneous discussion.

6. Don't judge. Let them "just talk," and accept what they say.

7. Take them seriously and validate their feelings. For some group members, this might be a rare or entirely new experience. Paraphrasing ("You felt she didn't understand"), checking ("Did I hear you correctly? You mean he...?"), asking for more information ("I don't think I quite understand..."), acknowledging feelings ("I can see how upset that made you"), or simply offering an "Mmmmm" in response to a comment shows that you are listening and want to understand.

8. Relax and let the group be more about process than product. It may not always be apparent that something specific has been accomplished, but as long as members keep talking respectfully and appropriately, you're on the right track.

9. Be willing to role model everything, but beware of sharing your personal experiences too often and in too much detail. Remember that this is *their* group, not yours. The role modeling you do should be for the purpose of facilitating student responses. Too much can *inhibit* response. You might not need to role model most of the activity sheets, especially if they are self-explanatory and if there are time constraints.

10. Be alert to moments when it is wise to "protect" individuals. For example, if a group member begins with something like, "I've never said this to anybody—it's about something pretty bad that happened to me...," you may want to encourage him or her to pause before continuing ("Are you comfortable about sharing this with the group?"). Ask the group, "Are you ready to be trusted? Remember what we said about confidentiality."

11. In situations where members of the group verbally attack each other, another kind of protection may be needed, namely leader intervention. The group can also process what has happened by sharing their feelings about the conflict.

12. If a student reacts emotionally, with intense discomfort or tears, offer verbal support, a tissue (if handy), or a touch (a pat on the arm, perhaps, or a hug) *if* the student has indicated that touch is all right. Encourage group members to offer appropriate support as well. Acknowledge that many adolescents wish that they knew what to do or say when someone is upset. Find out what is needed and wanted, and offer guidance to those who wish to offer support. Some students may ask to be ignored.

13. If conflict arises among members of the group, use the group process to deal with it. This is an excellent time to talk honestly about feelings and to demonstrate conflict resolution. Invite the group to tell how they feel about the conflict.

Facilitate communication among those in conflict. Check out whether each person feels heard.

14. Listen carefully to the student who is speaking, but also monitor nonverbal behavior in the entire group. Be alert to those who are not speaking. Are they showing discomfort (averted eyes, moving back, facial tics), frustration (agitation, head-shaking, mumbled negatives), or anxiety (uneasy eyes, unsteady hands, tense face)? You might want to check out those behaviors. What feelings are behind them?

15. Be honest and sincere in your comments, commendations, and compliments. Watch for and act on opportunities to tell students that they have done well, especially in articulating complex feelings and situations ("You put words on a very complex feeling." "You explained that very well").

endings

Each session includes a suggestion for closure. If you complete the session and the closure and still have time left over, you might use it to begin the next writing activity or to ask questions designed to encourage thinking about the next session. You can always use the time to talk more about the session just completed—about thoughts and feelings generated.

At the end of a group experience—whether a short series of sessions or an entire year of meetings—it is wise to wind down purposefully. The Final Sessions section includes two sessions you can use to conclude a series of meetings: "Planning Ahead: Wish Lists" and "An Informal Assessment."

Most important in any final session, and possibly over the last few sessions, is the need for participants to talk about what they have experienced in the group. I have also found that asking students to write a few paragraphs during a final session is helpful. Sometimes, when group attendance was voluntary, I have asked, "Why did you keep coming to the group?" At other times, I have simply invited students to talk about what they have gained in personal insights, what they have learned about adolescence in general, what areas of common ground they have discovered, and how they have changed over the period of time the group has met.

All groups, whatever their size and duration, need to prepare for the time when the group will no longer meet. Most students miss the group when it is done, and they feel a sense of loss. Especially if they have grown to depend on the group for support, they may feel anxious about facing the future without the group. If they have learned to know others well through the group, and if they have made friends, they may wonder if they will lose touch once the group disbands.

A few sessions prior to ending, mention casually that there are only a few meetings remaining. Continue to do that until the next-to-last session. At that time, you might mention what you have in mind for the final session, or ask the group for suggestions. You might plan a party, have food brought in, and/or take a group photo.

Be sure to leave time at the final session for them, and you, to say good-bye. If it is possible that they will not have much future contact, provide a way for them to share addresses and wish each other well. Be aware that you will be role modeling, and offering strategies for, ending what has likely been a profound experience. For many people—adults and teenagers—that is a difficult process.

It is not always easy to "read" a group and to know whether it is moving in a positive direction. Individuals who readily and frequently give feedback cannot speak for everyone. Quiet members may be gaining insights that they simply aren't sharing. A session that seemed to generate an indifferent or poor response might, in fact, have made an impact, but it may not have been apparent. Groups are complex, and members differ in their needs and what they respond to. Therefore, it is wise periodically to have group members fill out an evaluation, certainly at the end of the group experience.

On page 197, you will find a "Discussion Group Evaluation" form to copy and give to your group members. Or you might choose to create your own form, tailoring the questions to your group and to what you hope to learn. Feedback provided on such evaluations can be invaluable when assessing past groups and planning for future groups. This evaluation form has been placed at the end of the book, with the Final Sessions, but you can certainly ask your group members to do an evaluation every 8–10 sessions rather than waiting until the last day of the group experience.

17

permission for student participation

Dear Parent,

I have invited your son or daughter to participate in a discussion group at school. The purpose of the group is to provide adolescents with an opportunity to gain skills in articulating common social and emotional concerns. Such skills are important in all relationships—friendship, marriage, college roommate relationships, relationships with co-workers, and parenting. The groups are also designed to promote self-awareness during a period when young people are establishing their identity and preparing to move into adulthood.

Adolescence is a time of stress in even the best of situations. Not only are there physical changes; there are also new feelings and emotions to deal with. It is a time of increasing awareness of others' expectations. There are also new opportunities for involvement at school, and there are academic choices to be made. Relationships take on new dimensions.

Our discussion group will focus on social and emotional concerns. Even though we may discuss academics in terms of feelings and future plans, for example, the group will be far different from the often competitive academic world. Students will relax with each other and find out what they have in common. They will learn how to communicate support to each other. They will become acquainted with classmates in their group—for the first time, perhaps, or simply better than before.

If your adolescent participates, you may soon notice positive growth both at school and at home. There may be positive changes in communication. Talking about relationships, developing strategies for problem-solving, gaining a clearer sense of self, feeling the support of trusted peers—all of these experiences in the group should contribute to enhanced self-esteem and life satisfaction as your son or daughter navigates adolescence.

The group will begin very soon. If you give your permission for involvement, and if your adolescent decides to participate, please sign below and return this form to me as soon as possible. If you have any questions, please call me at _____.

_____ has my permission to participate in the discussion group.
(Name of child)

_____
(Parent signature)

_____
(Date)

group guidelines

The purpose of this group is to "just talk"—to share our thoughts, feelings, and concerns with each other in an atmosphere of mutual trust, caring, and understanding. To make this group successful and meaningful, we agree to the following terms and guidelines.

1. Anything that is said in the group stays in the group. We agree to keep things absolutely confidential. This means we don't share information outside of the group. We agree to do our part, individually and together, to make this group a safe place to talk.

2. We respect what other group members say. We agree not to use put-downs of any kind, verbal or nonverbal. Body language, facial expressions, and sighs can all be put-downs, and we agree to control our own behavior so that everyone feels valued and accepted.

3. We respect everyone's need to be heard. We agree that no one will dominate the group. We understand that just because someone is quiet or shy doesn't mean he or she has nothing to say. We also know that active listening and keen observation are valuable skills.

4. We listen to each other. When someone is speaking, we look at him or her and pay attention. We use supportive and encouraging body language and facial expressions.

5. We realize that feelings are not "bad" or "good." They just *are*. Therefore, we don't say things like "You shouldn't feel that way."

6. We are willing to take risks, to explore new ideas, and to explain our feelings as well as we can. However, we agree that someone who doesn't *want* to talk doesn't *have* to talk. We don't force people to share when they don't feel comfortable sharing.

7. We are willing to let others know us. We agree that talking and listening are ways for people to get to know each other.

8. We realize that sometimes people feel misunderstood, or they feel that someone has hurt them accidentally or on purpose. We agree that the best way to handle those times is by talking and listening. If someone feels hurt or misunderstood, we want him or her to express those feelings and explore where they come from. We encourage assertiveness.

9. We agree to be honest and to do our best to speak from the heart.

10. We don't talk about group members who aren't present. We *especially* don't criticize group members who aren't here to defend themselves.

11. When we do need to talk about other people—such as teachers and peers—we don't refer to them by name unless it is absolutely necessary. For example, we may want to ask the group to help us solve a problem we are having with a particular person.

12. We agree to attend group meetings regularly. We don't want to miss information that might be referred to later. Most of all, we know that we are important to the group. If for some reason we can't attend a meeting, we will try to let the leader know ahead of time.

an introductory exercise

Complete these sentences:

1. One feeling I have about starting this group is_____
   _____
   _____
   _____

2. I'm not sure what we'll do in this group, but I hope the group will_____
   _____
   _____
   _____

3. I'm glad that I can _____
   _____
   _____
   _____

4. I have a bad habit of _____
   _____
   _____
   _____

5. I have a good habit of _____
   _____
   _____
   _____

6. I'm glad someone taught me to _____
   _____
   _____
   _____

7. When I first meet someone, I _____
   _____
   _____
   _____

8. Something I consider valuable is _____
   _____
   _____
   _____

9. When I have time to do whatever I want, I usually _____
   _____
   _____
   _____

10. Something I'm proud of is_____
    _____
    _____

11. I'm probably most comfortable when I ____
    _____
    _____
    _____

12. Someday I'd like to learn to_____
    _____
    _____
    _____

13. A place that is special to me is_____
    _____
    _____
    _____

14. Someone I admire is _____
    _____
    _____
    _____

15. I know I can _____
    _____
    _____
    _____

focus
feelings

focus: feelings

Adolescents deal with intense emotions. Someone special pays attention. They are invited to a most important party. They get a good grade on a tough assignment. They get compliments on something they wear. They do well in gym class. They fall in love. These are the great times, when the ride is on the upswing. It's easy to smile and laugh and be lighthearted then.

But with other experiences, the roller coaster rolls downhill. The social climate at school can be competitive and volatile, and relationships change. Rough language may be aimed in their direction. They feel disappointed when things don't work out as hoped, and sometimes they feel devastated. They experience losses and transitions at home, and they grieve. They say and do things they know they shouldn't, and they feel guilt. They experience the rush of romantic love, and they suffer when relationships end. They also suffer if their parents' relationship ends, and they experience anxiety as parents remarry and families blend. They perceive that holiday celebrations aren't what they used to be. They aren't children anymore, and their family may have changed considerably.

Then there are the perplexing mood swings. Adolescents feel intensely, and they don't have the wisdom that comes from experience to know that nothing stays the same. Situations change. Time heals. Feelings pass. Sometimes they lose heart. They may flirt with dangerous behaviors and may become seriously involved. They probably worry about the future. Sometimes they show their feelings, and sometimes they don't. They might believe that no one feels as they do. Their distress can be lonely. Adults may not realize that insignificant events may feel like major traumas to a teen.

It's good to talk about feelings. Practicing that skill will probably help future relationships—with spouse, with partner, with children, with friends, and with co-workers. Learning to identify and accept feelings helps us to stay balanced in a complex world.

general objectives

- Students feel emotions in the present, affirm them, and talk about them with a group of supportive peers and a concerned adult.
- They look at past emotions and gain perspective.

focus: feelings
mood range

background

This session sets the stage for those that follow in this section. It is helpful to look at mood range. On a scale of 1–10, some individuals experience the full range, some a narrow 4–6 range, some a moderate 3–8 range, some a range that stays buoyantly above 5, and some a range that never rises above 5. It is interesting for students to consider their own and each other's fluctuations in morale, particularly during adolescence, when mood swings seem to be the norm. Do families have unique ways of expressing emotions? Do all people have intense emotions, but only some express them intensely? Do family members differ in mood ranges? Do we protect ourselves from 1s with narrow mood ranges that then rob us of 10s? These are questions to think about.

Compassionate parents want to protect their children from feeling bad. But such protection takes away opportunities to practice getting through bad times. Everyone needs to learn to deal with the self and the world. Preoccupation with keeping children happy can lead to children's fearing the "bad" and depending on others to provide stimulation and happiness. Children need to learn that it is all right to feel bad—and that bad feelings are survivable. One way to move past bad feelings is to feel them—to go through them. That can include talking about them. Much emotional energy is spent keeping the lid shut tight on uncomfortable emotions.

It can be beneficial for students to hear about others' mood ranges and about how they experience both lows and highs. This session also gives them an opportunity to express concerns about moods, including sadness and depression.

objectives

- Students learn that mood range varies widely within their age group.
- They consider that they might have some choice about their own range of mood.
- They consider how mood range may affect life, and vice versa.

suggestions

1. Go around the group, asking students what their mood is on a scale of 1–10 (1 is "very bad," 10 is "fantastic"). Invite them to comment on what might have contributed to their mood. You might want to spend

time discussing some of their situations, but be sure to allow time for each person to report. Even if only 5 or 10 minutes remain when this discussion seems to be winding down, go ahead with suggestion #2.

2. Ask questions like these:

   ▶ What is your usual range of moods, perhaps over one week's time? 1–10? 3–7? 5–9?

   ▶ What seems to send you up or down?

   ▶ How often do you swing up or down?

   ▶ Do you sometimes feel sad or depressed for no apparent reason?

3. Invite the group to think about who models mood range for them. Ask questions like these:

   ▶ Are you mostly like other family members in mood range—or are you different?

   ▶ Whose mood range is (most) like yours? Whose is (most) different?

   ▶ How do you feel about that person (those people)?

   ▶ Do you make your mood range different from theirs on purpose?

   ▶ How much control do you feel you have over your mood range?

   ▶ How do you usually feel about people who have a very different mood range from yours?

   ▶ What mood ranges do most of your friends have?

4. Prepare for closure with these questions:

   ▶ What were you thinking during the discussion?

   ▶ What were you feeling?

   ▶ Did any comment provoke strong feelings in you?

   ▶ Is there a variety of mood ranges in the group?

   ▶ Were you surprised by anything?

5. Closure can simply be a summary comment by you or brief comments by a few students.

focus: feelings
mood swings

- Students learn that mood swings are common in their age group.
- They feel less strange after listening to shared experiences and thoughts about moods.
- They practice positive self-talk as a way to cope with downswings in mood.

1. Ask the group what they have heard about mood swings during adolescence. They might mention the following:

   ▶ Mood swings seem to be fairly common during adolescence.

   ▶ Probably many things contribute to them:
     - rapid physical growth
     - hormonal changes
     - becoming more aware of and concerned about the other gender
     - changes and conflicts in the social scene
     - complex social relationships
     - becoming more aware of family stresses
     - the tug-and-pull of beginning to separate from parents and explore the world beyond the family
     - the bumpy process of finding out who we are as individuals
     - role models, and the family style of coping with stress.

2. Ask the group for suggestions about how to cope with mood swings:

   ▶ What do you do that helps you survive your mood swings?

   ▶ How are your parents coping with your mood swings?

   ▶ Have your parents come up with some strategies for dealing with them?

3. Pass out sheets of paper and ask the students to draw a line representing their moods during the past week. Some lines may be evenly and moderately rippled, some might have sharp peaks and

dips, and some might be almost flat. Invite the students to display their lines and describe the changes in their moods.

4. Introduce the idea of self-talk. Statements like the following—made to the self—might be helpful in coping with downswings. Saying and hearing them over and over can help to block out self-criticism.

   ▶ "I have a right to be imperfect."

   ▶ "I have a right to make mistakes."

   ▶ "(She/he/they) (has/have) a right to be imperfect."

   ▶ "I will feel better soon."

   ▶ "I'm really stronger than I feel I am right now. I'll get through this."

   ▶ "I've gotten through times like this before."

   ▶ "I'm learning."

   ▶ "They said adolescence was tough. I guess that's what this is."

   ▶ "I need to be patient (kind, gentle, understanding, tolerant) with myself."

   ▶ "I'm not alone. Others my age are riding this same roller coaster."

   ▶ "I'm okay."

   Invite group members to close their eyes and repeat silently one or two positive statements to themselves. If there is time, and if you think it would be helpful, go around the group first and ask which statement(s) might be most helpful for them—today or on a daily basis. No matter whether their mood is up or down at the moment, practicing positive self-talk can help them prepare for future situations.

5. For closure, ask someone to summarize the discussion. Ask these questions:

   ▶ How did it feel to talk about mood swings?

   ▶ Were you surprised by anything that was said? What surprised you?

   ▶ Was the discussion helpful? (Closed questions like this often elicit a few nods that provide a positive ending, especially when no time remains for further discussion. If there is no rush, make it an open-ended question: "What about the discussion was helpful?")

focus: feelings
unfair!

- Students focus on situations that seem unfair.
- They gain skills in articulating feelings about them.
- They have an opportunity to vent frustrations about the adult world.
- They practice seeing unfairness from a different perspective.

suggestions

1. Begin by asking the group to brainstorm—and perhaps list on a chalkboard—things in life that seem grossly unfair. Tell them you want to hear about situations, institutions, systems, or people that make them feel intense emotions about unfairness. (Be prepared for anything from school, court, corporate, and political systems to gender issues and the minimum wage for teenagers. Students might also mention specific actions by adults in their lives.) Then ask these questions about their list:

   - Are any of these the result of poor adult judgment?
   - Are any of these deep problems in society in general?
   - Do some seem unfair because they set limits—or have strict rules?
   - Are some of them unavoidable—i.e., "necessary evils" with no way to avoid them?

2. Change the direction of the discussion with some of these questions:

   - How do you react when things seem unfair? What do you feel?
   - What feelings cause problems for you?
   - Have your feelings ever harmed relationships?
   - How do you release your frustrations? Where?
   - Do you tell anyone how you feel? Who?
   - Do you eventually get over it, or does the feeling of unfairness go on and on?
   - How do you usually handle intense feelings?
   - Does the way you handle feelings work for you? How do you know?

3. Put unfairness into a somewhat different light, especially if your group likes to deal with the abstract. Ask these questions:

   ▶ How do you think "unfair" actions by adults can help you move into adulthood? (They give teens something to react against and to help them clarify their values. They give teens a chance to assert themselves and gain confidence.)

   ▶ What advice would you give to someone your age about how to deal with unfairness?

   ▶ What is a smart way to deal with unfairness? (Figure out how to get the system to work for you. Decide to let it go instead of dwelling on it. Find someone to talk to about it. Become a political activist. Talk directly to whoever is being unfair.)

4. Tell the group, "Most people would probably agree that it is the job of parents to set wise limits for their children. Protecting and nurturing means firm and consistent guidance and discipline. Children are owed that. With that in mind, consider these questions."

   ▶ Can you think of something "unfair" your parents said or did that turned out to be wise?

   ▶ Can you think of times when your parents were able to do something unpopular with you that was important for your safety or growth?

   ▶ Can you recall a time when a parent, relative, teacher, or coach made a demand of you that was unfair (and might have been an abuse of power over you)? How did you feel about that? How did you respond?

   ▶ Have you ever been given great responsibility as a child—for example, for taking care of the family, for making family decisions, for being a "parent" to others in the family (including being a parent to a parent), or for doing most household chores? If so, how have you handled that? What are your feelings about that? What have you learned through that? (Even though such situations represent an inappropriate family hierarchy, a child may perceive that there is little or no choice when assuming adult responsibilities.)

   ▶ How fairly or unfairly have the adults in your life treated you?

   ▶ Would you like *more* rules and limits in your life? (Preface this by saying that some adolescents do, in fact, wish for more guidance and limits. Invite the group to consider reasons for such wishes.)

5. Ask these questions:

   ▶ What are you owed as adolescents—by your teachers, by your parents, by your employers? (They may think this is just a manipulative question, meant to convince them that they are owed nothing. Quite the contrary. The adults who are responsible for them *do* owe them—care and nurturing, protection, and guidance.)

    ▶ Is it helpful to talk about fairness/unfairness? How is it helpful? (It can be helpful to find out what upsets others: two people with the same agenda might be able to change a situation. Even when situations seem unchangeable, there is less loneliness in knowing that others care and may have similar problems. There is benefit in learning how to put strong feelings into words. Sometimes that is how we find out what we think and feel. Maybe we don't know we feel something is unfair until we apply that word to it—and it fits.)

6. For closure, ask someone to summarize what has been discussed, or tell the group what you yourself have heard. Thank them for their honesty and helpful sharing, if that is appropriate. You might also ask the following questions:

    ▶ What did you feel during the discussion?

    ▶ What did you think about during the discussion?

Affirm the students as a group. Tell them, "You have a lot of potential as a group," or "It's good to see you developing as a group," or something more appropriate.

focus: feelings
disappointment

background

This session provides another chance for group members to practice articulating thoughts and feelings and to let down the protective facade that adolescents, like others, "wear" in order to present an image of ease and confidence and hide insecurities. All in your group have experienced disappointment, as all people inevitably do, and all have survived. It is usually not difficult for adolescents to recall long and short moments of disappointment. They will probably welcome the chance to hear others' stories and to hear how they coped. Perhaps they will recognize the value of learning to deal with disappointment—and of not having others protect them from it.

objectives

- Students articulate experiences of personal disappointment and express their feelings about those experiences.
- They recognize that disappointment is part of life.
- They learn that experiencing disappointment is instructive and builds resilience.

suggestions

1. Begin by asking, "What is 'disappointment'?" After group members have shared definitions and examples, ask them if they feel they have experienced it a lot, an average amount, not much, or hardly ever.

2. Encourage them to share moments of disappointment in their lives. First, ask them about disappointments in school—at any age, including the present. Then ask if they have had disappointments in friendships or relationships or at home. Questions like these might be appropriate for each area:

   ▶ How did you handle the disappointment?

   ▶ How did you react? What did you feel?

   ▶ How long did it take to move past the disappointment?

   ▶ What did you learn about yourself or about your feelings in the process?

   ▶ What did you learn about coping? What advice can you offer to others?

> Should someone have protected you from disappointment? (If the examples are related to academic, social, or not-being-chosen situations, or material wants, the answer is more likely to be "No." However, be aware that negligence by adults in their lives probably warrants a "Yes.")

3. If #2 didn't already move in this direction, ask the group members to think about possible effects of experiencing disappointment. Some might mention negative effects on motivation, self-confidence, faith in people, and trust in relationships, besides feelings of powerlessness and pessimism. However, others might speak of maturity, increased confidence from building resilience, increased drive to succeed, or compassion for others. Ask questions like these:

> When and how have you helped yourself get over a disappointment? (Perhaps they talked to a good listener, used positive self-talk or gave themselves a pep talk, immersed themselves in an activity, or tried again. Counseling is also a possibility.)

> Should we expect a life without disappointments? How much disappointment is normal? Can there be too much? Too little?

> What have you experienced in competitive school situations? What are possible results from always winning? From always losing?

> What can be gained through overcoming disappointment? (Perhaps define and discuss "resilience"!)

4. For closure, ask the group what has been thought-provoking for them during this session. Thank them for sharing, commend them for expressing their feelings well, and wish them a life with enough disappointments to help them build resilience and develop a can-do attitude.

focus: feelings
the light side up

background

Having a sense of humor can enhance life and help us to survive it. A sense of humor can mean having an eye for the ridiculous, the ability to respond with delight to comical situations, or the ability to laugh at ourselves. Humor can also be a way to cope. From the most grim childhoods can come nationally known comedians, joke-tellers in the break room at work, and nimble conversational wit. Laughter is helpful and healthful.

Use this session simply as a break from heavy topics, or use it to gain a serious perspective on the function of humor. Your particular group's needs and abilities should be your guide. If your group normally has difficulty sustaining dialogue because one or more "comedians" use humor to avoid serious conversation, you might prod group growth by addressing it as a serious topic. It also might be helpful and productive to discuss how humor can be hurtful. Sometimes other people's humor is uncomfortable, and we don't know why.

objectives

- Students appreciate the value and functions of humor in daily life.
- They explore their own sense of humor.
- They consider how humor can help people cope with difficulties.
- They consider how humor can be hurtful.

suggestions

1. Ask questions like these to begin:
   - Who do you know who has a sense of humor you appreciate?
   - What do you appreciate about that person's sense of humor?
   - How would you rate your own sense of humor on a scale of 1–10, with 1 being "nonexistent" and 10 being "terrific"?
   - Does your sense of humor show, or is it kept mostly inside— evident only in quiet chuckles or smiles?
   - Are you usually around people who have a good sense of humor?
   - What kind of sense of humor are you most attracted to?

32

2. Back up a bit. Pursue these strands:

   ▶ What is a "sense of humor"? (Does it mean joke-telling? Responding to situations? Making terrible, gross, uncomfortable things seem funny? Warmth and sensitivity? Comfort? Repartee? Dry wit? Practical jokes on people? Satire? Irony?)

   ▶ Describe your sense of humor.

   ▶ Do people learn to have a sense of humor, or is it natural?

3. Invite the group to consider the function of humor. Ask these questions:

   ▶ What can humor do for us? How can it help us? (It can help us cope with stress and relieve tension. It can help us not to take ourselves and others too seriously. It can provide a balance to seriousness.)

   ▶ Can you think of examples where humor (your own or someone else's) has been helpful for you?

   ▶ Can you think of examples where humor (your own or someone else's) has been hurtful? Offensive? A put-down? Critical? Can you remember a practical joke that caused great discomfort?

   ▶ Can humor sometimes interfere with, or shut down, conversation? Do some people use humor to lighten tense situations, or when emotions in a group seem dangerous? Can you think of examples of when this has happened? (Emphasize that there are times when it is preferable to let such emotions be expressed rather than covering them up and pretending them away.)

   ▶ What might be some good guidelines for telling jokes? (Be sensitive to those in your audience regarding gender, culture, age, religion, physical characteristics, socioeconomic status, and occupation—to name only some considerations. Never use humor to hurt or harm or make someone feel uncomfortable. Avoid jokes that callously demean any group. Use good taste and be discreet regarding the language and content of jokes.)

4. Ask if anyone has a joke to share. You might also ask the following:

   ▶ Is there a particular kind of joke that is popular with your friends lately?

   ▶ Do you enjoy hearing jokes? All kinds?

5. For closure, ask for a volunteer to summarize the session, or ask what was enjoyable, interesting, or thought-provoking. Did the discussion provoke any strong feelings? As your closing statement, affirm laughter as healthful, and humor as complex and interesting.

focus: feelings
anger

Anger is a powerful emotion. It is full of energy, and it demands attention and release. It can be expressed in violent outbursts, aggression, cruelty, or vindictiveness—but also undramatically and with quiet words. It can be expressed both effectively and ineffectively. It can hurt, and it can be perpetuated. It can find a voice in political and social action. It can also be bottled up, not articulated, stuffed, and turned into sadness and even physical and emotional problems when it goes on for a long time.

Anger can throw people off-balance. People can also be written off when they are angry too often and too intensely. Sometimes anger isn't allowed in a family. Many females, and, of course, some males, do not feel permission to be angry—or to express anger. Sometimes anger isn't even recognized as anger. It may come out in another form. The target of anger may not be the person or situation actually provoking it.

Anger can tell us a lot. If we pay attention to it, we can learn what we really feel. We can see why certain situations make us uncomfortable. Then we can do something to help ourselves. We can change something—if not the situation itself, then maybe our responses to it. We might ask for help from someone outside of the situation who can be objective. By understanding our behavior, and by learning to assess our feelings accurately, we can make anger a positive force.

The following, from page 1 of Harriet Goldhor Lerner's *The Dance of Anger* (HarperCollins, 1989), might be helpful as a backdrop for this session:

"Anger is a signal, and one worth listening to. Our anger may be a message that we are being hurt, that our rights are being violated, that our needs or wants are not being adequately met, or simply that something is not right. Our anger may tell us that we are not addressing an important emotional issue in our lives, or that too much of our self—our beliefs, values, desires, or ambitions—is being compromised in a relationship. Our anger may be a signal that we are doing more and giving more than we can comfortably do or give. Or our anger may warn us that others are doing too much for us, at the expense of our own competence and growth. Just as physical pain tells us to take our hand off the hot stove, the pain of our anger preserves the very integrity of our self. Our anger can motivate us to say 'no' to the ways in which we are defined by others and 'yes' to the dictates of our inner self."

Lerner stresses that it is important to clarify the source of anger and to express anger in productive ways, without feeling helpless and powerless and becoming defensive and attacking. She advocates clear communication and assertiveness. A discussion group can provide an opportunity to practice these skills.

recommended resources

Lerner, Harriet Goldhor, *The Dance of Anger* (New York: HarperCollins, 1989). A good resource for older adolescents.

LeShan, Eda, *When Kids Drive Kids Crazy: How to Get Along with Your Friends and Enemies* (New York: Dial, 1990). This wise, compassionate, and straightforward book can be helpful for all adolescents. The author addresses peer relationships through a multitude of anecdotes which make anger-producing situations and strategies for their resolution understandable to young readers.

Platt, Kin, *The Ape Inside Me* (New York: Lippincott, 1979). A short novel about a 15-year-old with a temper that affects his life in many ways. This believable, fast-paced story can be enjoyed by both middle school and high school students. It acquaints the reader with other adolescents as well whose feelings seem out of control and who eventually develop successful strategies for making changes.

objectives

■ Students learn to acknowledge and articulate feelings of anger and to recognize unresolved anger.

■ They learn that anger *is*—i.e., it is not something that one chooses or should/shouldn't feel.

■ They have a chance to speak about anger-producing situations—at home, at work, at school, or among their peers.

■ They learn that they have much in common with others their age regarding anger.

■ They learn that all *feelings* are okay, but not all *behaviors* are.

suggestions

1. Introduce the topic. Hand out copies of "Being Angry" (pages 38–39) and ask the students to fill out the questionnaire with brief responses, anonymously. Assure them that they will not be asked to share all of their answers. Then invite them to share whatever they are willing to.

   Encourage the group to respond, ask questions, and offer suggestions. You may want them to concentrate only on one of their situations— i.e., just "a" or just "b." If some members prefer not to share either one, they may ask to "pass" (which should always be an option). The group should not press anyone to share. Some may prefer to name the situation, answer "yes" or "no" to the other questions, and not elaborate. Fast readers may be able to "read down" all answers for "a," for example, in statement form ("It lasted a day," "Yes, it happens often," etc.).

2. Go around the group and invite each person to finish this sentence: "The time I was most angry in my life was probably...." They may elaborate on the intensity of what they felt, if they wish. Respect those who prefer to "pass."

3. Share with the group some of the information given in "Background." Encourage the students to read about anger, talk about it, understand it, and ask questions about it. Use some of the following additional thoughts about anger to generate discussion. Or make some of them into a handout for discussion.

    ▶ Anger is "energy." As a feeling, it is not immoral. We should pay attention to it. It can tell us what needs to be changed.

    ▶ We can channel anger constructively into competitiveness, such as in sales and athletics.

    ▶ We can channel anger constructively into political action, protests, social causes, and efforts to right a wrong that has hurt a person or a group.

    ▶ Destructive anger hurts people and things; constructive anger channels the energy into positive action.

    ▶ We express anger in many ways—silent withdrawal, moodiness, foul language, insults, criticism, manipulation, tantrums, and violence, for example. We can also use earnest, heartfelt, rational words.

    ▶ It is possible to be angry with someone we love. It is also easy to transfer anger to those who happen to be around—especially at home.

    ▶ We need to understand why something "pushes our anger button."

    ▶ We are frightened of our own anger. It threatens our sense of control.

    ▶ Learning how to deal with anger while we are young is important.

    ▶ Females may feel less permission than males in our society to be angry. They may feel sad when they should feel angry. Males may feel more permission to be angry than to be sad, and therefore may express anger when they feel sad.

    ▶ Talking about strong feelings with a good listener is helpful. If we can express feelings to someone who hears and accepts them, and if we feel heard, we can begin to move beyond those feelings. Talking about strong feelings with the target of the feelings is even more preferable. An objective third person may be needed to help, both to listen and to respond in helpful ways.

4. Ask, "Is there someone you are angry with often? Do you argue a lot or exchange angry words? Do you find yourself saying the same things over and over? Maybe there's a way to break that habit." Encourage

them to try something different next time. For example, instead of defending themselves or attacking the other person, they might respond by calmly saying, "I hear you. You're saying...." Point out that changing a pattern in this way is a personally powerful thing to do. When the other person feels heard, he or she might be more willing to listen in return. Eventually *both* people may feel heard, which can help to resolve conflict and diminish anger.

5. If time remains, ask, "How did you learn to 'do anger'? Did someone show you how?" (Some group members may propose that ways to express anger are "inherited." Ask them to consider instead that we learn how to "do emotions" by observation. This suggests that we can also learn new ways to express anger.)

6. For closure, have the students summarize the discussion, offer thoughts, or share feelings that surfaced. Encourage them to be alert to angry feelings during the coming week and to share observations at a later meeting. You might also conclude by asking which statements in #13 on the questionnaire they feel are true, especially if you have discussed anger in those terms. Collect and dispose of the questionnaires.

being angry

1. Briefly describe the last two times you were angry.

    a.   b.

For questions 2–12, your "a" answers should relate to the situation "a" you described in question #1, and your "b" answers should relate to situation "b."

2. What "caused" each situation?

    a.   b.

3. How did you act? (Did you say anything? Were you aggressive? Assertive? Did you do something physical? Hurt anything or anyone? Cry? Yell? Leave? Withdraw? Show your temper?)

    a.   b.

4. How long did your angry feeling last?

    a.   b.

5. Did you feel that something or someone was being unfair?

    a.   b.

6. Did you feel that you were being attacked or invaded or harmed somehow?

    a.   b.

7. Does this angry situation happen often for you?

    a.   b.

8. Is your anger about the situation done, or is it likely to come up again?

    a.   b.

9. Did you or someone else bring up "old garbage" that had nothing to do with the situation? If so, what?

   a.   b.

10. Was the anger connected to something that goes on and on, but is rarely discussed?

    a.   b.

11. Did you "talk out" your anger later with someone who was not involved in the situation?

    a.   b.

12. Have you discussed your anger with the person or persons involved in the situation?

    a.   b.

    If not, what would you like to say to that person or persons?

    a.   b.

13. Circle what you believe about anger. You may circle more than one response.

    a. Anger is one of many strong feelings that everyone feels sometimes.

    b. Anger is a bad feeling.

    c. Anger is a good feeling.

    d. Anger always hurts someone.

    e. Anger is always dangerous.

    f. Anger can be expressed in many ways.

focus: feelings
fear

It isn't just small children who are afraid. Adolescents—even in high school—can have great fears. They may fear certain school situations, like giving a speech, talking in a group, or having no one to eat lunch with. They may fear for their parents—for their safety, health, or job security. They may fear for their own health and may fear death by accident, AIDS, gang violence, or random shootings. They may fear the future—because it looks bleak and dangerous, or because it carries awesome responsibilities. They may fear abuse—and may even fear going home after school because home is dangerously unpredictable. They may have social anxiety—and anxiety about sexual orientation and behavior.

To discuss fears openly and honestly requires a safe place to talk. A discussion group that has had time to build trust offers a chance to share fears. Talking about them can help group members to cope with them.

objectives
- Students communicate honestly about their fears.
- They learn that others their age also have fears.
- They practice identifying and distinguishing between rational and irrational fears.
- They consider ways to diminish irrational fears.

suggestions
1. Hand out copies of "Being Afraid" (page 43). Have the group fill out the activity sheet, anonymously, as a way of tuning in to past and present fears. Depending on trust and age level, invite the students to share some of their responses—perhaps just #1, #2, and #3 if you think they might be hesitant to share the others. (For #1, they might mention bad dreams and barking dogs, heights and depths, fire and water, spiders and snakes, or being lost, for example.) Then ask questions like these:

    ▶ Have some of your early fears continued until today? Which ones?

    ▶ Were some of your early fears provoked by specific things that happened to you? What, for instance?

> What did you do when you were afraid?

> Did you have someone to comfort you? If so, who? If not, how did you feel then?

> Did any fears bother you at bedtime?

2. Move the discussion into the present. Choose questions from the following that are appropriate for your group's age, maturity level, and environment:

> What are your fears now?

> What do these fears feel like? (You might want to encourage similes and metaphors—like "heavy weights," "lurking monsters," "a hand around the heart," "a knot in the stomach.")

> When do you get "butterflies" in your stomach, or feel that your heart stops for a moment?

> Are some of your fears vague—about relationships, family, school, or the future? Would you be willing to share some examples?

> Do you worry about finances—your own or your family's?

> Do you worry about health—your own or someone else's? Are there family medical problems that cause fear?

> Do you fear violence—at home, on the street, at school? Do you often feel unsafe? Do you move through your day ready to run from danger, with adrenaline ready to pump?

Let the discussion move freely in any of these directions. Complex situations might come up, and sharing might be spontaneous and responsive. Encourage the students to communicate feelings. If they tell a story about something fearsome, move as quickly as possible past the event and ask them what their feelings were and are. Tell them to put words on the feelings. Focusing on feelings is practice for effective communication in relationships and for coping with stress.

3. Eventually ask the group members to list orally a few fears that are real—things that could really happen. Say, "These may be *rational* fears." Then ask them to list some fears about things that are not likely to happen. Say, "These may be *irrational* fears." Then ask these questions:

> When do you worry most about things that are unlikely to happen?

> Do these fears stop you from doing important things? What things? Do these fears make you sad? In what way?

> Do you think of terrible possibilities—catastrophes? Can you give an example?

> What could you do to make these fears smaller? (Talk to yourself in a positive and encouraging way; look at the fears and figure out why they are so powerful; label them as irrational.)

41

> ▶ If you have irrational fears, why do you feel you need to dwell on them?

> ▶ What would be different in your life if you didn't have irrational fears?

4. For closure, ask someone to summarize the discussion. Ask the group these questions:

> ▶ Was it helpful to divide your fears into rational and irrational categories?

> ▶ Was it helpful to hear about the fears of others? In what ways?

> ▶ Were you surprised to hear about others' fears? What was most surprising?

Thank them for their honesty, if appropriate. Collect and dispose of the activity sheets.

being afraid

1. As a little child, I often was afraid that

   a. _____

   b. _____

   c. _____

2. Later on, I had these fears:

   a. _____

   b. _____

   c. _____

3. Of the fears I listed in #1 and #2, these were *rational* (they could really happen):

   a. _____

   b. _____

   c. _____

4. Of the fears I listed in #1 and #2, these were *irrational* (they were highly unlikely to happen):

   a. _____

   b. _____

   c. _____

5. My *rational* fears at the present time (real fears of real, possible happenings) are:

   a. _____

   b. _____

   c. _____

6. My *irrational* fears at this time in my life (fears of things that probably could never happen) are:

   a. _____

   b. _____

   c. _____

7. Of the fears I listed in #5 and #6, these take up the most energy:

   a. _____

   b. _____

   c. _____

focus: feelings
love

To adolescents, as to all people, love is a mystery. It is powerful and volatile, and it is not static. It can energize, and it can enervate. It can cause pain and frustration as well as deep joy. It is often consciously sought, and yet that is often when it is not found. People differ in what they call "love." What is it? What is involved? Is love tough and resilient, or is it fragile? What does it need to survive? Does it need words?

Most people would probably agree that it is important in a relationship to convey feelings and thoughts in words. However, they would probably also agree that it is difficult to do that on a regular basis. Busyness and stress can interfere in any relationship. Time for talking isn't set aside. Through talking, people can share what is inside. Talking can lessen loneliness. It can let two lovers, friends, or family members know each other, instead of having to rely on assumptions. All relationships eventually have some degree of conflict, and talking can ease tension, even when it provokes momentary conflict. Talking can lead to healthy negotiation and compromise about everyday matters. That is why the discussion groups focus on learning how to talk—discreetly—about what is thought and felt.

objectives

- Students consider what love is.
- They consider how love affects our lives.
- They learn that love is dynamic and changeable, a process needing nurturing.
- They consider the importance of communication and respect in loving.

suggestions

1. Ask the group how they would define "love," based on what they have observed or heard in their lives.

2. Ask the students if there are many different *kinds* of love. Give them time to think about this. If the following are not mentioned, offer them as possibilities, along with others you can think of that seem appropriate for your group:

family	child-like
romantic	parent-to-child
child-to-parent	infatuation
long-term-commitment kind	respect-and-support kind
love for a pet	

If your group consists of young adolescents, you might want to focus on some of these, rather than on the romantic-love emphasis of suggestions #3, #4, and #5 below.

3. Depending on what the students bring up, pursue these strands:

   ▶ Does everyone long for love? What kind(s) of love? (Among many possibilities is the idea of "completing" ourselves through partnership with someone with qualities different from ours.)

   ▶ What, specifically, might you long for?

   ▶ Is it true that adolescents fall in and out of love continually? Do adults?

   ▶ How much does a preoccupation with love dominate an adolescent's life?

   ▶ What is the most important aspect of love? (Consider touch, talking, companionship, comfort, knowing that someone cares, support, security, sex, affection, partnership, respect, sharing the day, and being motivated to be kind and generous, among many possibilities here.)

   ▶ What impressions of love do we get from movies, television, and magazines?

   ▶ Can love be "ordinary"? Or does it have to be dramatic?

   ▶ Is there a difference between "being in love" and "loving"? If so, what might this difference be? (You might want to mention that in the United States, the media put a lot of emphasis on "being in love." We can probably safely assume that in Western cultures, most people associate marrying with "being in love." Suggest to your group that in many other cultures of the world, other issues play large roles in marriage. Family lines, class, clans, security, and the parents' choice of a partner for their child may far outweigh considerations of individuals' wishes, including "being in love.")

   ▶ Is there a difference between adolescent love and adult love? If so, what kind of difference?

- Can a loving relationship have conflict? (Certainly. And skills in conflict resolution are important for sustaining relationships.)
- Can loving someone sometimes hurt? If so, what is the hurt?

4. Ask the group to comment on these statements as they pertain to loving someone:

- "I would die if I had to be separated from you."
- "He's everything to me."
- "I'd give up everything for her."
- "He's my whole life."
- "She's all I've ever wanted."

Don't be surprised if most students do not question these statements. Suggest that in healthy relationships, people still have a sense of who they are as separate individuals. They can still nurture themselves and be supported by other parts of their lives. Self-worth is fragile and vulnerable if it is totally dependent on someone else's affirmation.

5. If the group consists of older adolescents, pass out paper and ask them to draw a "pie" representing the self, and then mark off the part of the pie that is absorbed in a love relationship. The size of the portion will undoubtedly vary. Afterward, ask these questions:

- In an ideal world—or an ideal relationship—what part of a person's life would be absorbed by love?
- When someone is totally absorbed or preoccupied by love, how might that affect other friendships, individual interests, goals, or self-care?
- How important are other friendships, individual interests, goals, and self-care to a happy, well-rounded life?

6. Introduce the idea of the connection between loving and talking (referring, perhaps, to some of the thoughts in "Background"). Then proceed with these questions:

- How important is it to talk about positive, loving feelings? (Mention that people vary in their opinions and beliefs about how much talking is necessary.)
- How important is it for you to "hear the words" in your love life or in your family?
- Have you ever improved a relationship with someone else by talking about feelings? Or did someone ever improve a relationship with you by talking about feelings?

7. For closure, ask someone, or a few, to finish this sentence: "Love is...." Then thank the group members for their thoughtful contributions to the discussion, and wish them the best of love in life.

focus: feelings
feeling lovable

background

This might easily be a light, upbeat session. On the other hand, for teens who have low self-esteem, or who might be in particularly difficult situations, it might be distressing. However, it has the potential for affirming personal strengths, especially when a group has established trust, and members are well enough acquainted to have credibility when giving positive comments about each another. Assess your group carefully when considering whether or not to include this session, and what suggestions to follow for discussion.

objectives

- Students affirm their own and each other's personal strengths and worth.
- They recall a time when they were at their best.
- They explore ways to recapture their best selves.

suggestions

1. Pass out sheets of paper and invite group members to write something positive, personal, and appreciated about each of the other group members. They might mention something about personality, warmth, kindness, acceptance of others, ability to listen, faithfulness in attendance, energy, creativity, insights, deep thinking, unusualness, assertiveness, sensitivity, smile, or eye contact, for example. Be aware that, especially if some group members have not been showing a positive side, it might be difficult for others to affirm them. Giving suggestions at the outset will help.

2. Holding the focus on one person at a time, invite the rest of the group to offer affirming statements.

3. Invite them to remember a time when they were probably their "best self." If your group prefers to write down ideas before sharing them, ask them to list a few of the characteristics of this "best self."

4. Ask each group member in turn to share the context of this positive period in their lives. Following are strands that may be followed if they don't appear spontaneously:

   ▶ How old were you?

   ▶ What helped you to feel so good?

   ▶ What messages were you hearing from others?

   ▶ How was the rest of your life affected by your being at your best?

   ▶ What were you doing for yourself at that best point in your life?

   ▶ If these best parts of yourself haven't been showing lately, where are they?

   ▶ What could you do (or what would help you) to bring your best parts to light again? (Encourage them to think about what they can do for themselves, rather than focusing on what others can do for them.)

   Suggest that the group problem-solve together for the last question, if that seems appropriate. Be careful, however, to validate whatever negatives they might bring up as preventing the best self from surfacing again. For example, you might say, "Yes, it sounds as if you're in a challenging situation right now"; "That sounds like a lot of pressure"; "Yes, sometimes it's hard to remember the best of ourselves when our world seems out of joint." Don't minimize the difficulties they are facing, but affirm the best part from the past. Be sure to remind group members that the best part was—and still is—part of them. Express confidence that they will be able to find it and use it again, especially since they have gained strength in managing difficult situations since then.

5. For closure, tell the group that it was good to hear about their best selves. Ask for summary comments about feelings or thoughts or the discussion in general. How was it to talk about this topic as a group?

focus: feelings
love and hate

Love and hate are huge topics that deserve more than a one-time discussion. The various topics in Focus: Relationships offer more opportunities to consider these two areas—and the fine line that divides them. They are a pair of emotions, experienced in connection with many kinds of relationships—and at all ages.

Adolescents often experience emotional "fusion" in romantic relationships, investing all of themselves and being totally absorbed, preoccupied—and possibly jealous and possessive. They may lose themselves in the relationship and may not have much of the self left when a relationship dissolves. It is not only hate that might then replace love, but also devastation and loss of self-worth.

This session does not necessarily have to discuss hate, even though it is certainly worthy of discussion. The main focus can be on dimensions of love—in all its complexity. The value of the discussion, no matter what direction it takes, is in the students' learning to articulate feelings and concerns. There are several discussion questions to choose from. For each, carefully assess maturity level and time constraints.

objectives
- Students learn about love and hate through exchanging ideas about them in a supportive group.
- They consider the difference between healthy and unhealthy romantic relationships and gain insights into their own experiences.

suggestions
1. Introduce the topic by asking these questions:
   - Have you ever hated someone you used to love? How was that possible? How do you explain that?
   - What was it like, moving from one to the other? Was the change sudden or gradual?
   - How can there be such a thin line between love and hate? (Suggest these possibilities, if group members don't mention them. Does it have to do with intensity? With trust and loss of trust? With loss of security? With two people "becoming one" and

49

losing their individuality? With hurt? It will help the discussion if they can refer to the situations mentioned in response to the first two questions.)

▶ What has happened to those emotions in you since then? Have they stayed the same?

2. Ask group members to consider situations when romantic relationships are less than healthy. Offer the following feelings and behaviors if the group doesn't mention them:

jealousy	the need for constant reassurance
possessiveness	fear of separation
demands for proof of love	preoccupation with the partner
dependency	dominance/submissiveness
selfishness	manipulation to keep the relationship going
self-deprivation for the sake of love	
insecurity	panic over separations
anxiety	little independent, personal space

If time permits, and if it is appropriate for the age level of the group, explore the idea that both love and hate can suffocate, control, or consume a person. Let the group brainstorm some ways to deal with such love or such hate. Insights from past experience and success stories might be helpful.

3. Especially with older students, explore what can happen when relationships dissolve. Let them share experiences or tell what they have observed. Ask these questions:

▶ Is the potential for hate, a desire to hurt, or depression greater when self-esteem is dependent on the relationship? What are you basing your opinions on?

▶ What can be done when a person suffers a traumatic break-up? (Counseling is an option. Remind them that counseling is really a lot like talking in a discussion group. Counselors have special training to be attentive, empathetic listeners and guides.)

4. Explore the topic of hate, making sure that there is adequate time to deal with thoughts that might come up. There will be no easy answers to the questions that follow. It is important to validate feelings that are expressed ("I can sense how intense that feeling is," "That's a strong feeling," "That's probably a scary feeling," "You just put words on a very complicated feeling. That's impressive"). Your responding calmly and supportively to group members' emotions will help the feelings seem less scary and more manageable. Ask questions like these:

- ▶ What is "hate"? Describe or define it.
- ▶ Is hate a comfortable topic to discuss? Why or why not?
- ▶ Is hate always "bad"? If not, can you think of times when it might serve a positive function? (Group members might consider whether or not it is beneficial to be able to hate abuse, injustice, or a particular trauma—or the person responsible. Hate might also be a stage in a healing process, one which will pass eventually. Whatever "hate" is, is it better than feeling depressed or victimized? What if hatred goes on and on?)
- ▶ Are you feeling hatred toward someone these days? (If school, social, or family situations are provoking hatred, focus on what individuals can do to feel in control of their lives again. Let the group brainstorm possibilities. Some group members might have valuable problem-solving strategies to share, based on past experiences. Suggestions might include changing their responses, choosing to "let it go," using self-talk like "I don't need to let him/her control me" or "I'm in charge of my life and I don't need to let hate govern me," or talking to a counselor. Emphasize that sometimes a trained helper is needed to help make sense of a situation.)

5. For closure, ask someone to summarize the discussion—or to define "love" and "hate," based on the content of the session. Ask, "How do you feel about the discussion? Was it helpful? Was it interesting?" If time is short, let nods suffice. If time remains, ask, "What was helpful? What was interesting?"

focus: feelings
happiness

background

I recall a poster about happiness that was displayed prominently in a room I once taught in. I don't recall the exact words, but it said something like this: "Happiness is like a butterfly. It escapes us if we chase it. But when we're not preoccupied with pursuing it, it may come and sit on our shoulder."

That's a nice thought. But many adolescents have doubts. Some wonder if happiness actually exists anywhere. Others, certainly, have felt happiness—maybe even often. They might not feel it every day, but they have faith that it will be there, like the butterfly, again.

"Happy" is a word that adolescents use often, whether describing the feeling of a moment, or telling how they wish they could feel. This session can move in many directions.

objectives

- Students learn that there are many ways to view happiness.
- They consider whether happiness is something to be achieved, whether it is a choice, whether it can be pursued, and whether it might sometimes be there, but go unacknowledged.

suggestions

1. Begin by asking, "What does 'happy' mean to you?" Encourage them to describe feelings and give examples of times they have felt happy. Ask these questions:

    ▶ Do success, love, security, quietness, contentment, rest, competence, weather, faith, friends, favorite activities, or gifts make you happy?

    ▶ Or is happiness not related to anything particular?

important

Be alert to those group members who might actually be saddened by a discussion of this topic. Some might be cynical and pessimistic about happiness. Encourage them to express their feelings. Give them "baking time" for complex thoughts. Validate their feelings.—i.e., don't express doubt about their feelings ("I can't imagine why you would feel that way"), but, rather, affirm their feelings ("That does sound sad." "I hear your frustration."). It is important that they feel heard and not squelched. If their thoughts affect the mood of the group, discuss that, but without judgment. Those who are not "happy," whatever that is, probably are aware of the power of their feelings and might be hesitant to speak. The group can practice listening attentively and affirming them.

2. Ask questions like the following after group members have expressed themselves:

   ▶ How often do you think about happiness?

   ▶ Are any of you usually buoyant and upbeat? (To those:) How much do you think about happiness?

   ▶ Do upbeat people think about happiness *less* than people who are *not* upbeat? Do unhappy people think about happiness a lot? Is that possible? What do you think?

   ▶ Does anyone here *not* think about happiness much? (To those:) But do you *feel* "happiness" fairly often? Not often?

   ▶ Do some of you feel distressed that you don't feel happiness often or at all? (To those:) Is happiness on your mind a lot?

   ▶ Can you remember times when you were happy? What was different then?

   ▶ What do you think helps (or would help) you to feel happy?

important

Be prepared for the mention of "altered states"—through drugs or alcohol, for example. If so, explore that kind of "happy"—i.e., short-term effects, escapism, danger, addiction, poor coping habits that are counterproductive. Sexual activity might also be seen as a route to happiness. Affirm that the sexual drive is certainly powerful and that it is fueled by feelings and desires for feelings. Group members might consider that sexual activity can also be a potentially dangerous way of coping with stress and pursuing happiness, especially if it is seen simply as a means to that end. It is important, if either of these areas come up, to hear their thoughts and opinions first before offering your adult views. Be aware that they will be watching your responses. Your responding rationally, without preaching, will provide them with the opportunity to express feelings, let down the facade, and be young and vulnerable. In some cases, that opportunity might be rare. It's always important to hear about the adolescent world and adolescent concerns, and not to make assumptions, before pronouncing adult opinions and advice.

3. Continue the discussion by asking questions like these:

    ▶ (After telling the group about the poster mentioned in "Background"): Do you think that "happiness is like a butterfly"? Do you think happiness can be pursued?

    ▶ Does happiness involve choice? Do you think a person can choose to be happy, even in bad circumstances? If so, what has convinced you of that?

    ▶ Can a person in a reasonably good situation choose *not* to be happy? If so, have you seen examples where this seems to be the case?

    ▶ Do you think people have habits about feeling happy or unhappy? If so, what are you basing your opinions on?

4. If someone brings up the topic of depression, the group might pursue that spontaneously. You probably will want to prepare yourself by reading through the "Sadness and Depression" session (pages 64–69) in advance of this session. If depression is not mentioned, that topic is best delayed.

5. For closure, ask someone to summarize the discussion, or ask one or more of the following questions:

    ▶ What have been the main ideas in our discussion today?

    ▶ Has the discussion caused you to think about happiness in a new way?

    ▶ What were your feelings during the discussion?

    ▶ Was this a good topic to discuss? Why or why not?

focus: feelings
coping with change, loss, and transition

background

Many situations and events involve loss: the death of a loved one; the death of a pet; the loss of a friend who moves away; the loss of a friend because of a move; the loss of childhood; the loss of innocence; the loss of security and trust; the loss of family "the way it used to be"; an accident, illness, or other situation that changes the ability to do favorite things; a relationship that doesn't work out; the shattering of an image (one's own or someone else's).

Grieving is certainly not just for losses through death. For every loss there is grief, which may or may not find a way to be expressed. And with every loss comes a time of transition: to life without the person, the pet, the place, the friend, the family the way it was, the trust, the relationship. The transition period may be uneven, as new resources and new rhythms are found.

This session gives students an opportunity to share experiences related to loss and transition. Perhaps they can find common ground, comfort, and hope through that communication. Not all members of a group will have experienced difficult transitions. However, those who have will probably feel support from the group, and those who have not will gain understanding and compassion for those who have.

objectives

- Students learn that many life experiences involve loss.
- They learn that it is helpful to share such experiences discreetly with others.
- They gain hope through hearing how others have successfully navigated transitions.

suggestions

1. Introduce the topic with material from "Background" or ask the group members to brainstorm life experiences that involve loss.

2. Hand out copies of "Experiencing Loss" (page 57) and ask the students to complete the questionnaire with very brief responses, anonymously. Use the questionnaire to generate discussion. You might take one part of question #1 at a time and ask for volunteers to share what they have written. Be sensitive to the fact that they might not feel

comfortable sharing several of the answers. Simply state that they can decide what would be appropriate to share.

3. In discussing the responses, ask the following questions. (If someone's loss is in the present, adjust the questions accordingly and omit the last two.)

   ▶ Do you remember your feelings at the time of the loss? What were some of them that you recall?

   ▶ Were you afraid of what would happen next?

   ▶ Were you afraid of your emotions?

   ▶ Did anyone give you support? Who?

   ▶ What was the hardest part of going through that experience?

   ▶ What did you have to learn to accept?

   ▶ What did you do for yourself?

   ▶ How long did it take you to move past the intense feelings of loss?

   ▶ What advice would you give to someone just beginning the same transition?

   For advice, you might offer the following suggestions, if the group doesn't mention them:

   ▶ Go ahead and feel.

   ▶ Try to understand that feelings help us to start going *through* a difficult experience. We can survive them. Feelings can be painful, but they move us forward.

   ▶ Talk to a friend or an adult—someone you trust. Or talk to a counselor. It can help.

   ▶ Find ways to keep going. Distract yourself. Keep busy with activities. Plan for life after your loss. Reach out to others.

   ▶ Remember that time *does* heal, though sometimes slowly.

4. Especially for groups with high ability, but certainly for others as well, mention that emotional sensitivity—and perhaps thinking too hard—can make some transitions in life difficult. Even normal transitions—the passage into puberty, high school, college, adulthood, or marriage— might be frightening and uneven. Each new stage can bring new and intense feelings of loss. There might also be exaggerated responses to traumatic personal or family experiences. On the other hand, high sensitivity and/or high ability might help them to deal with those times. Invite the group to share times when they have used their abilities or sensitivities to get past a rough time, perhaps through recognizing that feeling strong emotions was an important part of the process, or through using their mind to make sense of a complex situation.

5. For closure, you might ask a few students to summarize what they thought or felt during the discussion. Collect and dispose of the questionnaires.

experiencing loss

1. Have you ever experienced loss through...

   ...the death of someone you were close to?

   Yes ☐ No ☐

   Who? _____

   ...the death of a pet?

   Yes ☐ No ☐

   What was the pet's name? _____

   _____

   ...moving away from friends?

   Yes ☐ No ☐

   Who were they? _____

   _____

   ...having friends move away?

   Yes ☐ No ☐

   Who? _____

   _____

   ...losing trust in someone?

   Yes ☐ No ☐

   Who? _____

   ...losing trust in something?

   Yes ☐ No ☐

   What? _____

   _____

   ...an illness or accident?

   Yes ☐ No ☐

   What happened? _____

   _____

   ...a change in your family that made it
   different from what it used to be?

   Yes ☐ No ☐

   What was the change? _____

   _____

   ...the loss of a special friendship?

   Yes ☐ No ☐

   Who with? _____

   ...being disappointed in a special person?

   Yes ☐ No ☐

   Who? _____

   ...loss of innocence, or childhood, or the past?

   Yes ☐ No ☐

   Which one? _____

   ...the loss of feeling secure?

   Yes ☐ No ☐

   When? _____

   ...a major change in your life?

   Yes ☐ No ☐

   When? _____

2. Pick three of the circumstances described
   above. What feelings do you recall from that
   time?

   a. _____

   _____

   b. _____

   _____

   c. _____

   _____

   How long did it take before you felt better?

   a. _____

   _____

   b. _____

   _____

   c. _____

   _____

focus: feelings
when parents divorce

No matter what socioeconomic and cultural backgrounds are represented in your group, some adolescents probably will have experienced divorce in their families. Some might have experienced it several years before; some might be currently living through the uneven period that often follows it; some might be caught up in the throes of custody battles or the decision about which parent to live with. Feelings and behaviors related to separation and divorce may include loss of concentration, acting out, sadness and depression, anger, or sense of loss.

Divorce isn't abnormal or unusual today. Two-parents-together-forever families are less common than in the decades past, and anyone who portrays divorce as aberrant is out of touch with reality. Of course, divorce is not an ideal and should not be promoted as a preferred practice. But it is unfair and inaccurate to characterize all divorced families as unstable and broken—i.e., not functioning. It is also unfair and inaccurate to assume that all single parents are inadequate in child-rearing—or that all so-called "intact" families parent adequately. In many cases, divorce stops abuse and mutual destructiveness that even counseling cannot alter. Those who divorce and are finally able to address important personal needs and lessen their vulnerability to abuse are undoubtedly healthier than they were before. People can do harm by staying together, too.

What are some possible reasons for the high divorce rate? Media messages foster unrealistic expectations about marriage. Our mobile society deprives us of the support of extended family and old friends. As a society, we are not adept at communicating personal needs in our relationships. Couples grow and change in different ways, at different speeds, and too few go for counseling early, when problems start to surface.

Often, young adults marry without first forming separate identities and clear ego boundaries. When something goes wrong, they are unable to deal with imperfections in themselves or their partners. They cannot look at the relationship in parts and address those that need fixing. People who are not healthily separate individuals tend to form and leave relationships quickly. They continue unhealthy patterns that are familiar to them and that reflect their poor self-esteem. They are not committed to changing those patterns, and often they lack the skills needed to change them.

Whatever the reasons for a divorce, it is never easy on those involved, particularly the children, who likely don't receive the same benefit as the adults. How children cope and thrive following a divorce depends on the parents and what they do to help avoid the protracted tensions that occur when the *emotional* divorce is left unfinished. Sometimes divorce escalates conflict instead of stopping it, with rancor and vindictiveness going on for years. Long and expensive court battles are hurtful for everyone involved, since the focus stays on what is wrong. Mediation or work with *both* legal and mental health professionals can help make the process less destructive. When parents can maturely separate spousal issues from parental issues, they can better keep the children in mind in the midst of the stress of divorce.

There are many similarities between death and divorce in how people react. Divorce means change, change means loss, and loss means grief. Grief needs mourning, a process that might take years. It is important to feel the feelings rather than push them away, since they can remain toxic and affect the future if they are not allowed to run their course.

It is important to help children of any age understand that good people do divorce, that children are not responsible for parents divorcing, that it is difficult when they are asked to play messenger between Mom and Dad, that it is easy to idealize the absent parent and have conflict with the custodial parent, that proper preparation for divorce can lessen many fears in children, that even adult children can feel devastated by their parents' divorce, and that the need for co-parenting after a divorce doesn't necessarily end when children grow up. Under most circumstances, children deserve some sort of consistent contact with both parents.

Adolescents might find normal confusion about sexuality exaggerated by divorce. In addition, children of divorce sometimes are afraid of marriage, stay tenaciously in unhappy marriages, or repeat patterns from the past. Discussion groups can help them learn important communication skills, encourage honest exploration of feelings, and ultimately help to prepare them for long-term relationships.

important

Some group members might welcome a discussion of divorce; for others, it might be painful. Especially when the group has not been organized specifically for "divorce support," you will need to be sensitive to various situations in addressing this topic. You might even give general permission at the outset for students to remain silent during the discussion. Even those who are uncomfortable with the topic might benefit from sitting in on the discussion.

The comfort/trust level of the group, how long ago or recently group members have been affected by divorce, and the number who have been affected will likely determine how much, and if, students share and interact during this discussion. During the previous session, in order to know what to expect, you might have them tell you on paper if their parents are divorced, and, if so, when the divorce occurred; if they are in a "new family"; how they feel they have been affected by divorce; and if they are willing to talk about their feelings and experiences in the group. Explain that you will be addressing the topic soon, but that they will be in charge of whether they share anything about their experiences, and that you will not ask them about divorce unless they indicate their willingness to be asked. Mention that those who have not been affected by divorce might learn more about it and become more sensitive to those who have, and that everyone can benefit by sitting in on a discussion and hearing what others have to say.

If your group is large, or if it consists of an entire classroom, it might be more difficult for students to share their thoughts and feelings regarding this sensitive and emotionally charged topic. In fact, this topic may not be appropriate for interactive discussion in a large group. Consider a presentation by you or someone else instead.

objectives

- Students learn about how young people respond to divorce.
- They learn how children of divorce adjust to their altered families.
- They learn that it can be helpful for children of divorce to share feelings about their experiences.

suggestions

1. Familiarize yourself with the information given in "Background" and organize an introduction to the topic that is appropriate for your group. Acknowledge the inevitable changes and loss that result from divorce; perhaps mention general dilemmas for children regarding divorce; note that adjustments to new family and living situations take time; assume that the divorce probably remains a significant memory; and affirm that good people sometimes have difficulty living together. You might even refer to how common divorce is in your school or institution, since many children in divorced families are unaware of that and feel that no one can understand their situation. In a comfortable small group, support from those who have "been there" can be valuable for those experiencing divorce in the present.

2. There are many different strands you might pursue to initiate the discussion. If you followed the suggestion in "Important," you might say, "Last time, some of you wrote that you have experienced divorce. If you are willing to share some of your experiences, your thoughts might help others in the group to better understand what divorce means." If some group members have indicated that they are willing to share, ask the following questions:

   ▶ How did various members of your family react to the divorce?

> How did you react?

> What roles did your family members have before the divorce? For example, who was the leader? Helper? Bill-payer? House-cleaner? Dishwasher? Car-fixer? Family organizer? Any other roles?

> Did roles change because of the divorce? In what ways?

> Have you been given new responsibilities since the divorce?

> Did the divorce come as a surprise to you?

> Have you gone through stages—of adjustment, attitudes, feelings?

> How would you describe those stages?

> What kind of contact do you have with the parent who doesn't live with you?

> What have you learned about yourself in this experience?

> What strengths have you discovered in yourself?

> What advice would you give someone going through divorce now?

Ask the group members who are willing to share if others may also ask them questions, especially those who are in need of assurance or advice. It will be your responsibility to encourage discretion ("Think carefully about your questions, and be sensitive to feelings and the need for family privacy") and, if necessary, intervene ("Is that question too personal?"). Some answers might generate helpful discussion.

3. For closure, thank the group for sharing and for offering support, if that is appropriate. Remind them that talking about feelings is important for healing and also as practice for their own relationships in the future. In order to get feedback for yourself and future planning, ask them if the discussion was helpful, comfortable, and important.

focus: feelings
dealing with holidays and family gatherings

After (not before) a holiday break from school, one involving family get-togethers and anticipation, this topic can help students tie up some feelings about what they experienced and address some of the developmental issues that are involved. Holidays bring out the best and the worst in extended families. They also bring into sharp focus the adjustments required when families break up, are re-formed in new configurations, or are joined by new in-laws in the family circle.

Adolescents sometimes feel caught in the middle at gatherings, suspended as they are between childhood and adulthood. Perhaps they cannot just happily play with the cousins, as they used to, because they have grown up and have different interests. Maybe they are not interested in the adult conversation either. The traditional holiday event just doesn't have the wonder and color that it used to. In addition, older adolescents often work too many hours at their jobs over the holidays. Perhaps they have to travel to one parent's distant home—and meet his or her new spouse. Holiday get-togethers may be painful reminders of how things used to be.

This session can be valuable for gaining perspective. Expect a variety of experiences and feelings —from "best ever" to "worst possible."

objectives

- Students learn that any frustration or sadness they experienced over the holiday break was probably shared by several others their age.

- They put their feelings into a developmental perspective.

- They learn to articulate the complex and varied feelings that are experienced during the holidays.

suggestions

1. Have the students begin by reporting how they are feeling at the present moment on a scale of 1–10, with 10 being "terrific." They might give some reasons for their emotional state. This is a good way to direct attention to feelings, since that is the focus of the session.

2. Ask the students to tell about their vacations—what was fun, what was stressful, what new experiences they had. Or have them list on paper one or two times of good feelings in any context, and one or two moments of stress, and share some of these.

62

3. Move the focus to interactions with family members. If some individuals in your group celebrate at times other than during this season, encourage them to think back to the last extended family gathering they experienced. Ask questions like these:

   ▶ Which relatives attended your family gatherings?

   ▶ What kinds of relationships do you have with them?

   ▶ Do you see them often otherwise?

   ▶ What were some changes in them since the last time you were together? Had your feelings toward them changed?

   ▶ How would you describe your extended family? Do you usually have a good time together? If so, who is particularly enjoyable, and what kinds of things do you do together?

4. Focus on the feelings generated by group members' holiday experiences. Ask these questions:

   ▶ How did you feel at these gatherings? Happy? Sad? Giddy? Disappointed?

   ▶ Did you feel nostalgia? Love? Affection? Gratitude? Excitement?

   ▶ Were any feelings connected to major differences from the past? (Examples: loss of childhood, loss of the "old family," loss of familiarity, loss of "place," loss of a relative)

   ▶ Did you feel stress from "too much family," too many work hours, or adjustments to new family situations?

   Encourage group members to give examples or situations for each feeling they identify, but respect any reluctance to share. Affirm that the holiday world usually isn't neat and perfect, just as families are not.

5. Ask, "How would you describe the perfect holiday for you? Which family members would it include? Which family members would it exclude, and why? What would you do? What wouldn't you do?"

6. Steer the discussion toward growing up—and what that means in terms of making adjustments to the holidays.

   ■ Were the holidays different for you this year compared to last year because of your age?

   ■ How were *you* different?

   ■ Was there a difference in what interested you?

   ■ Were you treated differently from in the past?

   ■ Did you behave differently?

7. For closure, ask someone to give a one-sentence summary about school breaks and family gatherings, based on what has been shared during this session. Were there any discoveries or insights about adolescent experiences? Were there common feelings and experiences?

focus: feelings
sadness and depression

background

Only in the last few decades has the topic of depression been so freely discussed. What used to be largely closeted has been much researched in recent years, with significant breakthroughs in its treatment. Advances in the understanding of brain chemistry and the chemistry of stress have led to a number of effective drug therapies. Cognitive therapy that works to change the way people think about themselves and situations in their lives has also been effective. People still experience depression, and much of it goes untreated, but more are getting help now than ever before.

Like many adults, adolescents use the term "depression" loosely. Sometimes they use it for "being in a bad mood." Perhaps they are referring to a normal, situational unhappiness that will diminish with time. Or they might use it to indicate a moderate level of clinical depression characterized by fatigue, changes in sleep patterns and weight, physical pain, difficulty with memory, withdrawal from friends, lessened interest in favorite activities, and a general feeling of hopelessness. At this level, they might also "act out." As they try to improve their mood, but the depression remains, they can become vulnerable to peer pressure to use alcohol and other drugs. With severe depression, there are thoughts of suicide.

Because mood swings are so common during adolescence, it is difficult to know when to be concerned about depression. It is also hard to recognize the early signs. Because young people are so concerned with remaining socially acceptable, they often keep smiling, even when in emotional pain. They know it is difficult for others to be around a depressed person. There is a tendency for others to withdraw, just when focused attention is crucial. In addition, adolescents are often reluctant to ask for help. When they do ask for help, they may be disappointed. Others might respond, "All you need to do is get up and get on with your life," or "It doesn't make sense for you to be depressed when you have so much going for you." But for the clinically depressed, there is little or no energy to move ahead, no matter what others say.

There seem to be several varieties of depression, according to current thought. They include a mild, chronic category; minor and major depressions; depression associated with an event or situation; cyclically recurring depression; low periods that alternate with highs; and even a depression involving a perpetually gloomy and negatively critical outlook. Clinical assessment of depression usually includes questions about frequency, duration, and severity. Treatment varies, depending on the kind and level. *It is important that anyone with "depression" be checked out by a professional if it is interfering with normal life.* Depression may also be a sign or result of physical illness, and whatever factors are involved, it is important to treat it early.

Depression is escalating in the dominant culture in the United States, and it is common in Western cultures in general (Klerman & Weissman, 1989). The fact that females suffer from serious depression at a higher rate than males may be in part because females pay greater attention to moods and dwell more on depressing interpretations of events around them (Nolen-Hoeksema, 1987). Males may distract themselves with activity, but male alcoholism may be equivalent to depression in females, the result of society's giving the genders different "permissions." Females could learn from males how not to dwell on their emotions, and males could learn how to deal with negative feelings in a healthy way, instead of, for example, with aggression and violence.

Research has come to mixed conclusions about whether individuals with high ability are more prone to depression than others. Methods of identifying the gifted vary, and research samples may include only those who perform well in school, a sometimes challenged criterion for giftedness. But a significant body of literature affirms that hypersensitivity in the highly able might make them especially vulnerable to depression (see "Recommended Resources" below and on pages 71–72). Certainly they are not exempt from it and probably suffer from it at least as much as others. Discussion groups for gifted students should include this topic as much as any other groups should.

All adolescents need a safe, trusted context for talking about this common condition. Those who struggle with depression may find comfort in knowing that they are not alone and perhaps will ask for help. Those who have not experienced it can have their awareness raised. Assess the maturity and trust levels of your group when deciding if, and how, this topic should be addressed. It is most appropriate for older adolescents, although depression can occur even at very young ages. The format is most appropriate for small groups, rather than for full classrooms. If you decide not to use this session with your group, use the information in it to raise your own awareness.

recommended resources

For group leaders interested in learning more about depression:

Capuzzi, D., and Gross, D.R., eds. *Youth at Risk: A Resource for Counselors, Teachers and Parents* (Alexandria, VA: American Association for Counseling and Development, 1989).

Klerman, G. L., and Weissman, M. M. "Increasing rates of depression." *Journal of the American Medical Association,* 261, pp. 2229-2235 (1989).

Nolen-Hoeksema, S. "Sex differences in unipolar depression: Evidence and theory." *Psychological Bulletin,* 101 (2), pp. 259-282 (1987).

Piechowski, M. "Emotional giftedness." In N. Colangelo and G.A. Davis, eds., *Handbook of Gifted Education* (Needham Heights, MA: Allyn & Bacon, 1991).

You might also want to check back issues of periodicals like *Psychology Today* for articles related to depression.

objectives

- Students become more knowledgeable about depression.

- They learn that ups and downs occur in everyone and are part of growth, change, and life in general, but feelings of depression should not be treated lightly when they interfere with normal activity.

- They learn how to articulate feelings and thoughts associated with being "down."

suggestions

1. Introduce the topic by connecting it to stress, which is related to depression. The first few sessions in the Focus: Stress section of *Talk with Teens about Self and Stress* might be helpful in preparing for this session.

    If you don't have a copy of *Talk with Teens about Self and Stress* available, you might find the following paragraphs from page 151 of that book helpful for beginning a discussion of stress:

    "Mention the word 'stress' to an adolescent, and you will have begun a serious conversation. Starting at an early age, most young people become well acquainted with the high stress of living in this culture. Parents bring home the stress of the workplace, or they suffer job loss, both of which have a ripple effect on the family. Because ours is a mobile society, there are moves and dislocations that can cause stress. There are pressures at school, with some children coping well—and some not so well—with the demands of the system and the challenges of the social world. There may be illness, accidents, or other dramatic events that cause physical and emotional repercussions for months or years. For gifted students, their multipotentiality may cause stress. There are simply too many possible directions from which they may choose.

    "Stress is part of life—from growing up to growing old, facing change, facing illness, working, and caring for family members. Pessimism, trying to respond to everyone's needs, multiple responsibilities, and isolation all can heighten stress levels.

    "Consciously or unconsciously, families teach children coping skills. Some learn healthy and effective ways to cope with life's stressors. They talk about the stress they are experiencing, step back and gain perspective on stressful situations, and apply problem-solving techniques. They release tension through a healthy level of exercise, socializing, relaxation, diversion, or a deliberate change of pace and pattern. Others learn less healthy ways to cope with stress. They try to escape or deny it through alcohol and other drugs, overeating, workaholism, moving to a new location (the 'geographical cure'), sleeping, daydreaming, or watching too much television. Some resort to tantrums or violence in the form of abuse. Others 'cope' by blaming, scapegoating, punishing, or accepting a 'victim' posture."

Ask the following questions:

- ◗ What thoughts did you have as I read these paragraphs?
- ◗ Do you feel stressed a lot? About what?

2. Use parts of the "Background" for this session to provide information about depression, or invite a local mental health professional to speak to your group. You might want to do further reading on depression in preparation for this session. When dealing with topics like this one, it is important not to claim to be an authority unless, in fact, you are. Resist the impulse to share examples from your own personal history. Instead, you can introduce information by citing sources, and you can remind the group (if this is the case) that you are simply a layperson who is interested in depression and feels it is important to raise awareness about it.

3. Hand out copies of "Feeling Bad" (page 69) and ask the students to fill out the questionnaire with brief responses, anonymously. Explain that they will not be sharing the whole questionnaire with the group. When they finish, strongly emphasize that anyone who has been feeling deeply sad over a period of time should see you individually for suggestions about getting assistance. Give them specific times when you are available. Tell them that if they don't feel comfortable coming to see you, they should see someone else.

important

You are probably a mandatory reporter, and you will need to follow a proper procedure for notifying appropriate resources if someone seems to be suicidal. (See "Handling Emotional Bombshells," pages 12–13.) It is appropriate for you to ask students if they have thought about hurting themselves and if they have a plan in mind. If you are working in a school setting, and if you are not a particular student's counselor, see the counselor *immediately* if there is any cause for serious concern.

4. Use the questions from the handout in a sort of "poll-taking" manner, asking questions like these:

- ◗ How many of you have felt "down" in the last year? The last month?
- ◗ How many of you sleep more (less) when you feel "down"?
- ◗ Who gets depressed for no apparent reason?

The discussion is less invasive if you don't insist on an answer from everyone. (Then no one needs, self-consciously, to "pass.") Be aware that the answers to #4, #5, #7, and #8 might reveal symptoms of depression (see the second paragraph of "Background").

important	If the discussion leads you to believe that someone is in danger, follow up individually, outside the session, as soon as possible. Ask, for example, "Are you okay? Let's talk a few minutes about the mood you were describing today. I'm concerned."

5. Ask the group these questions:

   ▶ What do you think adults understand about teenage stress?

   ▶ Do people your age often assume that everyone else "has it all together"? Do you often feel that way?

   ▶ Does the high incidence of depression among adolescents today reflect anything about this time in our society? If so, what? (Life is more complex and confusing today. We're less patient with problems. Media messages, rapid and dramatic changes in society, and the incidence of divorce contribute to feelings of insecurity.)

   ▶ How much do you think small children understand during times of grief and family stress?

6. For closure, ask the students for summary statements, or contribute statements of your own. What was learned? What was felt? Was it good to talk about depression? If time is short, let nods suffice here. If time remains, ask, "Why or why not?" Collect and dispose of the questionnaires.

feeling bad

1. Have you felt significantly "down"...

   ...in the last year?   Yes ☐ No ☐

   ...in the last month?   Yes ☐ No ☐

   ...in the last week?   Yes ☐ No ☐

2. What seems to get you down? _____
   _____
   _____
   _____

3. Do you sometimes feel bad for no apparent reason?   Yes ☐ No ☐

4. Do those feelings change your sleeping?   Yes ☐ No ☐

   Do you sleep *more* than usual?   Yes ☐ No ☐

   Do you sleep *less* than usual?   Yes ☐ No ☐

5. Describe "feeling down." How does this feeling affect you?_____
   _____
   _____

6. How long does the feeling last? _____
   _____

7. Does there seem to be a cycle to that feeling (for example, every 2 weeks, once a month, every spring, every January)? If so, explain:_____
   _____

8. Does this feeling interfere with school?   Yes ☐ No ☐

   With your job?   Yes ☐ No ☐

   With relationships?   Yes ☐ No ☐

   If so, explain how it interferes: _____
   _____

9. What do you do to combat feelings of sadness? _____
   _____

10. Have you ever talked to someone about feeling sad?   Yes ☐ No ☐

    If so, who? _____

11. Have you ever written about feeling sad—just for yourself?   Yes ☐ No ☐

    Have you ever written about it for someone else to read?   Yes ☐ No ☐

focus: feelings
adolescent suicide

background

Suicide is near the top of the list as a cause of death among adolescents and young adults. Obviously, this topic should be included in any program focusing on adolescent affective needs. However, many adults are fearful of bringing up the subject—even with those students who are clearly suicidal. The adults may have a vague awe of the depth of feeling that precipitates suicidal thoughts, or they may be wary of what they themselves might have to handle if they begin a dialogue on this heavy topic. Teachers, parents, and even counselors often harbor a concern about "planting the idea" in those who may be "just depressed," and they also worry about the possibility of cluster suicides when there has already been one. Though understandable, those concerns should not preclude discussion of this important topic.

Contributing to thoughts of suicide in adolescents in general are family problems, loss, abusive relationships, relationships breaking up, sexual and other physical abuse, earlier abuse that rears its head with increased sexual awareness, homosexuality, and alcohol and other drug abuse. When several of these factors converge in a student's life, hopelessness can set in. No matter what the situation, those who contemplate suicide feel that there are no other options. They might not want to die, but they feel that nothing will change, and that life is too painful as it is. Young students don't have an adult's perspective. They may not believe that change is not only possible, but inevitable.

Students with high ability are no less vulnerable to depression—and therefore to suicide—than others. Anonymous, informal written surveys of my discussion groups of gifted achievers and underachievers from grades 7–12, spanning several years, have consistently found that more than one-fourth had seriously considered suicide for more than one day at a time. Other research supports such findings (see "Recommended Resources"). Heightened sensitivity to stress and feedback from others, especially about expectations, may be a factor in the suicide risk of high ability students. In addition, their emotional maturity might not match their intellectual level. They may struggle with existential questions and social justice issues that most of their age-peers are not bothered by. They may be highly self-critical, and their feelings may be treated lightly by others. Their defenses

70

may be so intact, and their emotions so controlled, that no one recognizes that behind even order and achievement may be vulnerability when social and emotional difficulties arise.

Discussion groups are an ideal forum for discussing the troubling phenomenon of suicide, which can usually be seriously and productively addressed if there is a good level of trust. Adolescents do not treat the subject lightly. Many have been around suicidal peers or family members or have experienced frightening thoughts themselves. They may have known someone who died from suicide. Assess the age and maturity level of your group carefully as you decide whether or not to address this topic. Certainly it must be handled sensitively if you do—and yet in a matter-of-fact and undramatic manner. Your ability to be calm and respectful in discussing this topic with them will be appreciated, and it will model that such topics can be discussed. That knowledge might be crucial someday. Wise peers can also be an important line of defense for troubled individuals.

important

One option (strongly recommended) for this focus is to invite a mental health professional to speak to, or be interviewed by, the group about depression and suicide. Another option is to do the same with a suicide survivor who is concerned about helping others cope. You will need to make arrangements in advance for either option. Suggestions for direction in interviewing a survivor are found in #2 below. The mental health professional might also discuss experiences in counseling that relate to these areas.

Be aware that individuals in your group may have been close to suicide or to a suicidal person at some point. They might not want that called to anyone's attention, since it still may be seen as shameful, or it may be too recent to be discussed comfortably. Be sensitive to the fact that they might not want to talk about it—and might prefer not to remain in the room for the session. You might want to give the group these permissions matter-of-factly at the outset. If some students leave, respect their wishes and reassure them that you look forward to having them back next time. Follow up with them individually, ask about their circumstances, and offer assistance, if appropriate.

recommended resources

For group leaders who want to learn more about suicide:

Delisle, J. R. "Death with honors: Suicide among gifted adolescents." *Journal of Counseling and Development,* 64, pp. 558-560 (1986).

Hayes, M. L., & Sloat, R. S. "Suicide and the Gifted Adolescent." *Journal for the Education of the Gifted,* 13(3), pp. 229-244 (1990).

Simmons, L. "Adolescent suicide: Second leading death cause." *Journal of the American Medical Association,* 257, pp. 3329-3330 (1987).

For group leaders and adolescents to share and discuss:

Gootman, M.E., Ed.D. *When a Friend Dies: A Book for Teens about Grieving and Healing* (Minneapolis: Free Spirit Publishing, 1994).

Nelson, R.E., Ph.D., and Galas, J.C. *The Power to Prevent Suicide: A Guide for Teens Helping Teens* (Minneapolis: Free Spirit Publishing, 1994).

For additional resources, check the counseling offices at your school.

objectives

- Students are exposed to information about suicide.
- They learn that even sad and scary topics like this one can be discussed.
- They learn that it is important to ask for help when feeling depressed.
- They learn that they should seek help for suicidal persons they may be around.

suggestions

1. This session should follow "Sadness and Depression" (pages 64–69), unless suicide was significantly addressed during that session. Introduce this topic with some ideas from "Background." A few points from the first paragraph might be appropriate for beginning the session, particularly the incidence of suicide among adolescents and the fear of discussing it.

2. If you invited a suicide survivor or mental health professional to this session, group members might ask that the visitor address some of the topics listed here:

   ▶ when the depression seemed to begin and what seemed to contribute to it

   ▶ when thoughts of suicide began

   ▶ what relationships with parents and friends were at the time

   ▶ whether anyone noticed the signs

   ▶ whether counseling had been considered or had taken place

   ▶ when and if counseling began afterward

   ▶ if there was hospitalization and what that involved

   ▶ when the turning point toward stability occurred

   ▶ what was/has been learned in counseling

   ▶ if there was a problem with anger, what coping strategies were/have been learned

   ▶ whether there were re-entry problems when returning home or to school

   ▶ whether teachers were aware of the difficulties, and whether that was good or bad

- whether there were changes in relationships after the attempt
- how to deal with a depressed person, based on personal experience
- how others can help regarding feelings of isolation
- how others can show concern
- whether the attempt involved a wish to be gone permanently
- whether feelings such as revenge or a wish to punish were involved
- suggestions for visitors to the hospital or to the home when someone has been/is suicidal
- what strengths were relied on during recovery
- the importance of dealing with problems
- what causes growth after a suicide attempt (Does suffering cause growth? Does growth occur when a person moves into new awareness?).

3. You might share the following pertinent information, perhaps with an overhead transparency, with a handout, or simply by reading the statements slowly, pausing between each one:

- Isolation and alienation contribute to suicide, but the key factor is depression.
- Suicidal thoughts are usually relatively temporary in one's lifespan. Eventually the despair is likely to fade away completely.
- Easy access to drugs, the glamorizing of death by the media, an unrealistic view of death (not fully realizing that it is permanent) by teens, pressure to succeed, and lack of family cohesion all might contribute to the increase in teen suicides today.
- Warning signs of severe depression, and consequent thoughts of suicide, include changes in behavior, appetite, sleeping patterns, school performance, concentration, energy level, interest in friends, attitude toward self, risk-taking, and a preoccupation with death.
- Most people who attempt suicide send signals first, such as comments about hopelessness or worthlessness, increased isolation, making arrangements for pets or possessions, or changing suddenly from agitation and depression to peace and calm (because the decision has been made).
- Anyone who suspects that someone is suicidal should ask direct questions about whether they have thought of killing themselves, or whether they have a plan in mind.
- It is imperative that anyone who feels that someone is in danger should act immediately to notify someone who can properly evaluate the situation and help to set up an appropriate support

73

system and/or referral for professional help. This holds true for adolescents, too, when they are aware that a peer is suicidal.

▶ Listening, accepting, and hearing the feelings are keys to helping a suicidal person. If the person is talking about desperate feelings, he or she is asking for help and hoping for change.

▶ Promises of confidentiality cannot be kept when a situation is life-threatening.

▶ Suicide is a permanent solution to a temporary problem.

▶ Suicide devastates the lives of the surviving family and friends.

4. For closure, ask students to summarize the session, or do that yourself. Or ask them whether it was helpful to discuss this topic. Let nods suffice. This topic often leaves groups quiet and deep in thought.

eating disorders

background

We live in a society obsessed with being thin. Advertisements equate thinness with sex appeal, store mannequins resemble only a few rare individuals, a multitude of diets are hawked loudly, and food products are promoted with the weight-conscious in mind. The upside to this is an awareness of fitness and of the nutritional value of various foods. The downside is that a society of young women—and, unequally, men—may stunt their growth, develop eating disorders, or have vitamin deficiencies.

Adolescents hear the media messages and food ads. Added to these are the comments that fathers, boyfriends, brothers, and other significant persons make to growing females. If a family overemphasizes appearance as a value at a time when a girl's normal growth conflicts with that value, the foundation for an eating disorder may be laid. At a time when their bodies should be growing normally, too many late-elementary girls today are dieting, because of their great fear of gaining weight and being unattractive. Many high school girls are obsessed with thinness. Their role models in movies and in fashion ads are now underweight.

What results too often is an eating disorder, especially in those who are culturally, biologically, or psychologically vulnerable. Chronically dieting, addicted, chaotic, neglectful, violent, over-protective or perfectionistic families; fathers who tease about weight; early dieting; a childhood history of obesity or sexual abuse; personality or impulse disorders—any of these can make someone vulnerable. Eating disorders usually begin during adolescence and can go on indefinitely. Discussion groups are a good place to raise awareness and sound the alarm.

High-achieving, perfectionistic, nice, compliant females are among those at risk. Perhaps they don't feel permission to rebel in the usual adolescent ways. Dependency and difficulty with problem-solving, trust, and intimacy may be factors, as well as being unable to express anger. Low self-esteem and feelings of powerlessness may also contribute, with the eating disorder then exacerbating the low self-concept.

Males also need to become aware of the problem, not just because they comprise a small percentage of sufferers, but also because they may have girlfriends, sisters, mothers, or friends who are in need of help for eating disorders, and because their comments have an impact. Athletes in certain

75

sports are also vulnerable, as are dancers. They are likely to suppress anger and to have high expectations and a high tolerance for physical discomfort. It is good to raise awareness about compulsive exercising or excessive dieting for athletics, since negative lifelong eating habits may become well established during years in school athletics.

Eating disorders may reflect power and control issues, difficulty expressing uncomfortable feelings, anxiety, fear of maturity, dependency, difficulty with problem-solving, and childhood trauma that damaged self-esteem, among many factors. Eating disorders are complex, and individual and family therapy is usually basic to recovery, the time required varying with the factors involved. Such disorders can become life-threatening. A distorted body image can drive the condition until heart failure, decreased kidney function, elevated blood pressure, stroke, cardiac arrhythmia, rectal bleeding, loss of normal intestinal function, electrolyte imbalance, enlarged salivary glands, dental enamel erosion, seizures, or depression and suicide may result, the medical consequences varying with the type of disorder (see "References" below).

As you discuss this topic with your group, offer these definitions:

- *anorexia nervosa:* self-starvation and an intense fear of obesity that does not diminish with weight loss; distorted perception of actual body weight, size, or shape; weight loss of at least 25% of original body weight. Almost all anorexics are female.

- *bulimia:* recurrent binge eating of high-calorie foods, probably inconspicuous, followed by depressed mood or self-deprecating thoughts; probable purging or highly restrictive diets, using vomiting, laxatives, or diuretics; frequent weight fluctuations greater than 10 pounds. Most bulimics are female. (See "References" below.)

Before discussing this topic with your group, take advantage of resources in your school or local library or counseling center to become more informed about eating disorders. Acquaint yourself with local or regional resources where eating disorders are treated. You might also be able to obtain some brochures from a medical or mental health facility to distribute to the group.

important

One option for dealing with this topic is to invite a local expert on eating disorders to make a presentation to the group, with discussion following. You will need to make arrangements in advance.

The purpose of this session is definitely not to do therapy with those who may suffer from eating disorders. In fact, it is highly unlikely that group members will reveal even that they are worried that they might have a serious problem. As a general admonition, simply encourage group members, if they are worried, to seek professional help immediately if they have concerns about themselves, and to seek help for anyone they know who seems to have an eating disorder. Encourage individuals to see you privately for referral possibilities, and have resources available.

references

American Psychiatric Association. *Diagnostic and Statistical Manual of Mental Disorders: DSM IV* (Washington, D.C., 1994).

Donovan, D.M., and Marlatt, G.A., eds. *Assessment of Addictive Behaviors* (New York: Guilford Press, 1988).

Zraly, K., and Swift, D. *Anorexia, Bulimia, and Compulsive Overeating: A Practical Guide for Counselors and Families* (New York: Continuum, 1990).

objectives

- Students become better informed about eating disorders.
- They explore some possible contributing factors to eating disorders.
- They consider how social pressures might promote eating disorders in young people.

suggestions

1. If you have invited an expert on eating disorders to make a presentation to your group, follow the presentation with discussion.

2. If this will be entirely a discussion session, introduce the topic by asking what the group knows about eating disorders. Caution them against mentioning anyone by name, even though a personal experience or an experience of an acquaintance may have provided general knowledge that can be shared. Supplement what they report with material from "Background."

3. Students might want to digress into these areas:
   - societal pressures regarding appearance
   - expectations from families and boyfriends
   - concerns about control in life
   - the incidence of eating disorders among highly capable, achieving students.

4. You may want to offer additional information during the discussion, if you think it would be helpful:
   - The "ideal weight," by American standards, has become lower and lower over the past 20 years.
   - Women need a fat level of approximately 22% of their body weight in order to menstruate normally.
   - Bingeing is the body's natural response to excessive dieting. The more one diets, the more one feels the need to eat. The best defense against binge eating is to eat—and to eat sensibly, healthfully, and regularly.

5. For closure, offer some kind of summation appropriate to the session, or ask group members to summarize the discussion.

focus
family

focus: family

The family is usually our first environment. That environment teaches us about life, instills values, provides a context for learning social skills, and provides a base for exploring the outside world. Of course, families differ. Some are great nurturers, and some are destructive. Some are full of overt conflict, and others rarely raise voices or tension levels. Some adapt well when new situations arise, and some don't. Some families are emotionally close, and some are emotionally distant from each other. Some families talk easily and well, and some have difficulty sustaining conversations—or are simply not inclined to talk. Some have experienced great trauma, and some very little. Some must worry about providing basic needs, such as food, clothing, and shelter, and some never have to worry about these essentials. And there are families all along the continuum in each of these areas.

No matter what a family is like, it strongly influences a child's personal development. Family patterns influence whether a child trusts others, expresses anger (and expresses it appropriately), lives optimistically or pessimistically, has empathy, is concerned about global issues, and is successful at school. Whether any child, even one with disabilities, becomes an emotionally healthy person depends to a large extent on how well the family nurtures that child.

Adolescents are in the process of trying to figure out who they are within the family unit and how to become appropriately and increasingly autonomous with age. That process affects the way family members interact with each other. Sometimes relationships are strained even before a child enters adolescence. Sometimes there is little tension even during adolescence. It can be assumed, however, that the expected gradual separation process, as the child grows into adulthood, will contain stress and strain for those involved. Group discussion can be an effective way to deal with those family stresses during adolescence.

Many sessions in this section include questionnaires or activities. Always assess the questions carefully to determine whether they are appropriate for your group. You might want to alter wording, eliminate some of the questions, or simply use the handouts orally as discussion starters. Several of the handouts offer great potential for extended discussion. Instead of collecting and disposing of them at the end of the session, which is what I usually recommend, you might choose to collect and keep them for continued discussion during the next session.

For those students who indicate general discomfort with the topic, stress the information in "Important" and perhaps meet with them individually. Encourage them to participate as a way of dealing with family-centered stress.

important

"Family," for purposes of discussion, includes anyone who lives (or lived) together and may include grandparents, aunts and uncles, cousins, married older siblings, and even pets. It may also include persons in more than one household in cases of divorce and remarriage, especially when a child's time is regularly divided among them. "Extended family" usually refers to whatever generations of the family are still living, whether or not they live near each other. "Nuclear family" usually refers to parent(s) and children, although in today's circumstances that term might have a variety of meanings.

Depending on their cultural heritage, family traditions, and family situation, group members may have different perceptions of what a family is and what "family" means. It is important to be sensitive to, and accepting of, *all* group members' situations and perceptions of "family." Some may even speak of close friends as family and may not want to speak at all of blood relatives they feel cut off from. A discussion group is a good place to increase appreciation for diversity. Emphasize that various types and perceptions of families are simply different, not better or worse.

general objectives

- Students gain a more complex understanding of their families.
- They think about their place in the family context.
- They gain insights that might help them deal with family transitions, family conflict, parent-child tensions, separation issues, sibling interaction, boundary-setting, and parents.

focus: family
each family is unique

objectives

- Students become more aware of what is unique about their family situation and what they have in common with others.
- They consider that family interaction can include extended family.
- They affirm one or more members of their extended family.

suggestions

1. Introduce the topic with comments based on "General Background."

2. Hand out copies of "Family" (page 83) and ask the students to fill out the questionnaire with brief responses, anonymously. Suggest that they skip any questions they can't answer quickly.

3. Use the questionnaire to generate discussion. Ask all students to share what they have written for one question at a time, or simply ask for a few voluntary responses to each. Discussion can center on a few or all of the questions. Some may provoke a considerable exchange of ideas and experiences. Even if the discussion of this topic doesn't become spontaneous and interactive, rest assured that just sharing written responses represents a good level of self-revelation and contributes to group-building. In fact, even if you have time to discuss only a few items, group members will have benefited from quietly pondering all of the questions.

4. For closure, you might summarize the session, or ask one or more students to do this. Ask about feelings generated by the discussion in general or by specific comments. Compliment the students on their ability to express themselves, and thank them for their willingness to share with the group. Collect and dispose of the questionnaires, or keep them until the next session if you will be continuing the discussion then.

family

"Family," as the word is used here, means whoever lives with you in the place (or places) where you live. It also includes older sisters and brothers who have moved away from home. It may include other individuals as well. If you are not living with your birth family, you may choose to include both your birth family and the family you are now with, or just one of the families.

1. Describe your family—in whatever way you like. For example, you might write the names of your family members. Or you might describe the type of family you live in—traditional, single-parent, blended, extended, adoptive, foster, or whatever seems to fit. Or you might just list some words that you feel describe your family. _____
   _____
   _____

2. What do you like most about your family? _____
   _____
   _____

3. What do you like least about your family? _____
   _____
   _____

4. Who is your favorite family member? _____
   Why? _____

5. Which family member are you most like? _____
   How are you alike? _____

6. Do you live near your extended family (cousins, aunts, uncles, grandparents, etc.)?   Yes ☐ No ☐

7. Do you share good times together?   Yes ☐ No ☐
   If so, give an example: _____

8. Does your extended family give your family emotional support when
   there are problems?   Yes ☐ No ☐
   If so, give an example: _____

9. Who do you admire most in your extended family? _____
   Why do you admire this person? _____

10. How well do you know your extended family—the family members who are still living? _____
    _____

11. On a scale of 1–10 (10 is "a lot"), how much does your family celebrate holidays, birthdays, and other special events? (Consider the following: How many people in your extended family get together for these events? How much are these events planned and discussed? How much are these events referred to later as "historic moments"? How much are these events significant memories from your childhood?) _____

focus: family
family values

background

Politicians, churches, and other institutions and groups often speak of "family values," usually in a positive light. Depending on the context, family values might refer to the value of the family in general, traditional family structure, high moral standards, or what is right and good. Frequently, separate values are not specified.

This session looks at family values as reflected in how a family interacts socially and how it feels about work, play, change, tolerance, religion, and the news, to name just a few areas that reflect values. It may be both helpful and interesting for the adolescents in your group to think about their family values in these areas and to see how the family priorities expressed in the group differ.

objectives

- Students consider what is important to their families.
- They think about how much their own personal values are like or unlike those of their families.
- They learn that attitudes and values vary within their group.

suggestions

1. Introduce the topic and ask the group what they think of when they hear someone refer to "family values." They will probably have a variety of associations and/or definitions. Explain that the focus for the session will be "values," but the discussion might involve more areas than they usually think of when considering "family values."

2. Hand out copies of "Family Values" (page 86) and ask the students to complete the activity, anonymously. Use the statements to generate discussion.

3. As an alternative, you might use "Family Values" to do a continuum activity (which involves no writing and no photocopying sheets of paper). Have the students line up along one wall of a room (or form an angle along two sides). Tell them that they have just formed a "continuum." Designate one end of the continuum as "10–a lot" and the other end as "1–not at all." Explain that you are going to read aloud a series of statements about family values. After you read each

statement, the students should physically move to the point on the continuum that best represents where they feel they belong.

For each statement, ask two or three students to explain why they placed themselves where they did. If time is short, do this only for selected statements. (NOTE: This is the kind of activity that needs to move along quickly, and it is best not to spend too long considering individual statements.) Expect that there may be more than one way to interpret each statement. Some of the statements may generate discussion.

4. For closure, ask one or a few group members to name some common values in their group. Or ask what thoughts and feelings the discussion or continuum activity provoked. Remind the group that there is value in learning to recognize and talk about our values. It is one of many ways to learn about ourselves.

family values

Read each of the following statements. For each, ask yourself, "Would my family agree or disagree with this?" Rate the statements from 1–10, with 1 meaning "They wouldn't agree at all" and 10 meaning "They would agree strongly."

_____ Being social is important.

_____ Work is good—it feels good, and it offers more benefits than just money.

_____ It is important to know what is going on in the news.

_____ Parents, not others, are responsible for giving their children moral guidance.

_____ Parents should communicate their moral values to their children clearly, strongly, and often.

_____ Everyone needs a balance of work and play.

_____ Having fun at home with your family is better than depending on outside sources for entertainment.

_____ It matters what the neighbors and other people think of us, so appearances matter—our clothes, house and home, cars, friends, etc.

_____ It's good to be creative. Unusual creations deserve respect and support.

_____ The arts are important—music, dance, painting, drawing, theater, etc.

_____ Risk-taking is good—socially, personally, on the job, financially, and in play. It's best _not_ to play it safe and sure.

_____ Being physically fit is important.

_____ Family privacy is important. What is said and done within the family should stay within the family.

_____ A family should solve its own problems and not ask others for help.

_____ It's a family leader's responsibility to decide how to solve family problems.

_____ Eating healthfully is important.

_____ Athletic ability is important.

_____ Being associated with a faith community is important (church or synagogue membership, for example).

_____ It's best to put the past behind you.

_____ Change is good—and desirable.

_____ The more experiences a person has in life, the better.

_____ Being tolerant of others' lifestyles and beliefs is important.

_____ Achievement is very important, whether in school, at work, or in the community.

_____ Getting a good education is important.

focus: family
family communication style

objectives

- Students learn that families differ in the ways they communicate.
- They recognize that people usually learn to communicate in the context of the family, and that adults model how to make requests, offer help, show affection, encourage or discourage, express anger, vent frustration, and share the day's events.
- They consider how their own families communicate.
- They practice effective communication by role-playing problem situations.

suggestions

1. Introduce the topic by explaining that family communication can take many forms—words, both oral and written; hand and other body gestures; physical demonstrations of affection; symbols; gift-giving; phone calls; and smiles and frowns, to name several.

2. Hand out copies of "Family Communication" (page 90) and ask the students to fill out the questionnaire with brief responses, anonymously. You might choose only a few of the questions for discussion, or rewrite the questionnaire with fewer questions, depending on the level of maturity, ability, and trust in the group. In the interest of time, you could ask, for each question, "Who said 9 or 10?" or "Who said 3 or 4?" Then invite one or more group members to explain their response or give an example.

   Try to respond to each comment in a way that validates and affirms the feelings expressed ("I can feel your emotion when you say that." "I can hear that that's important to you." "That came from the heart, didn't it?"). Avoid judgmental statements ("You have no reason to feel angry." "I can't understand why you would feel that way." "Gratitude would be much better than anger." "Your strong reaction doesn't make sense").

   Emphasize that families differ in the ways they communicate, and that what works for some families might not work for others. There is no right or perfect way to communicate. Rather, what's most helpful is to consider how *effective* a particular communication style is for getting

87

needs met and for doing what needs to be done. Avoid ranking the quality of family communication competitively. Recognize that expression of affection, for example, may differ among cultures and among families. Of course, ideas for enhancing communication may come out of the discussion. Simply providing an opportunity to think about and discuss this broad topic is valuable for adolescents.

3. As an alternative, you might use the questionnaire to do a continuum activity. Not only do some groups like to move around, but bold answers through physical movement may have more impact than spoken numbers. Keep in mind, however, that any format can lose its appeal.

   Have the students line up along one wall of a room (or form an angle along two sides). Tell them that they have just formed a "continuum." Designate one end of the continuum as "10–very/a lot" and the other end as "1–not/not at all." Explain that you are going to read aloud a series of questions about family communication. After you read each question, the students should physically move to the point on the continuum that best represents where they feel they belong.

   For each question, ask two or three students to explain why they placed themselves where they did. If time is short, do this only for selected questions. Move this activity along quickly, and don't dwell too long on one question. Expect that there may be more than one way to interpret each question. Some of the questions may generate discussion.

4. If anyone mentions a high-stress situation, encourage the individual to express feelings about it, and recognize that just bringing it up may represent courage. The student might also be testing the group for response—to check out whether the group can handle hearing about the situation, whether it is too awful for discussion, or whether the group will pass judgment on it. It is appropriate to thank the student for sharing and compliment him or her for putting words on a difficult situation. Simple statements can affirm the student ("That must have been hard for you and your family." "That must cause a lot of stress and frustration.") The group might even be willing to do some problem-solving for the student. As always, allow anyone to "pass" on any item.

5. Hand out copies of "Family Communication Role-Plays" (page 91). Explain that the group will be acting out some or all of these situations. Divide the group into pairs or small groups and assign the roles. Discuss each role-play after it has been presented, and invite the rest of the group to offer suggestions for more effective communication. When appropriate, have the students role-play both negative and positive interactions.

6. For closure, stress that any conversation and communication within the group is good practice for later relationships—relationships with roommates, co-workers, spouses, partners, or children. If they can learn to talk about what matters to them, what they feel, and what worries them, they will be better able to ask for what they need, to express support and concern and affection, to work out problems in relationships, and to share the news of their day. Collect and dispose of the questionnaires.

family communication

On a scale of 1–10, with 10 meaning "very" or "a lot" and 1 meaning "not" or "not at all," rate your family on each of the following questions:

_____ How well do family members communicate with each other?

_____ How often does your family eat a meal together?

_____ How much conversation is there at mealtime (on the occasions most members are there)?

_____ How much is arguing a part of your family's communication?

_____ How well (positively, supportively) do family members deal with their own mistakes?

_____ How well do family members deal with each other's mistakes?

_____ How critical are family members of each other?

_____ How good are family members at listening to each other?

_____ How much do family members express anger (in any form—"good" or "bad")?

_____ How free do members of your family feel to express emotions?

_____ How clear-headed is your family, in general, when there is a crisis?

_____ How easily do family members compliment each other?

_____ How much do family members use words (instead of actions) to communicate personal feelings and wishes?

_____ How well can your family talk comfortably about difficult topics, including feelings?

_____ How openly affectionate are family members with each other?

_____ How well do you think you know what each family member thinks and feels?

_____ How much communication is there with extended family?

Answer these questions:

Who are the *most* talkative members of your family?

_____

_____

_____

In what ways do the *least* talkative members of your family communicate their needs?

_____

_____

_____

family communication role-plays

1. You have been losing sleep because someone in your family is making too much noise when coming home late at night. Talk to that person, using I-statements ("I've been feeling...," "I need...," "I feel...," "I'm concerned..."). Try to avoid putting the other person on the defensive. Speak of your needs or preferences.

2. You have a need for more privacy at home (for example, for sleeping, studying, or just being alone), and you've come up with an idea you'd like to try. Talk to the family at mealtime about your suggestion and your need for a change. Use I-statements ("I've been feeling...," "I need...," "I have an idea for how I could...," "I'm concerned...").

3. It is difficult for your family to give compliments to each other. You want to tell a sibling that you are proud of something he or she did recently. Talk to the person, expressing your feelings and asking for further details of the situation.

4. You just dropped a bottle of syrup on the floor and made a mess. Your entire family is there. Interact with your parent(s) about the incident. (Perhaps role-play a negative, escalating reaction, as well as an acceptance-of-error reaction.)

5. You are terribly angry about something your brother (or father, mother, sister) has done. Interact with that person. (Perhaps role-play a negative, escalating reaction, as well as one involving positive I-statements about feelings and clear statements about anger. For a positive result, try to speak about the deed and its effect on you, not about the person. Avoid statements that begin, "You always..." or "You never....")

6. Come up with your own real-life situation to role-play.

focus: family
family roles

objectives

- Students learn to appreciate the various roles that family members play in the family.
- They think about how personal needs are met and not met in the family.
- They recognize that roles might be altered—with effort.

suggestions

1. Introduce the topic and ask the group to consider these statements:

    ▶ Members of any family play various roles in that family.

    ▶ You undoubtedly play some roles in your family.

    ▶ There are probably both advantages and disadvantages for you in having those roles.

2. Hand out copies of "Family Roles" (page 94) and ask the students to fill out the questionnaire with brief responses, anonymously. Use a few or all of the items to generate discussion. You might simply have each person, in turn, "read down" one column of responses, then have everyone do the same with the second column, and then the third column. Stop after all have completed one column and ask if they heard anything surprising about anyone in the group, given that person's usual behavior in the group. People often are not the same at home as they are socially.

3. Ask the group if they have ever thought about this: Sometimes, even though we might *despise* how one family member behaves, we might *let* that person take care of an emotion or a behavior for everyone else. For example, one person might be responsible for all of the anger in the family, or all of the sadness, responsibility, seriousness, emotion-alism, rebellion, or risk-taking in the family. Explore this issue further by asking the following questions:

    ▶ What would happen if all members of your family were equally serious—if everyone shared that characteristic, not at an extreme level, but at a moderate level? What if all members of your family were equally angry? Equally sad? Equally responsible?

- How would that affect the person who currently "does all (or most) of the anger" (and so on) in your family? (Could that person maybe relax a bit, knowing that *everyone* could express anger that was justified, or that *everyone* could be lighthearted sometimes, or that *everyone* could feel sad about a sad situation, or that not just one had to be responsible?)

- How would it affect various individuals in the family if various emotions were expressed equally by all family members? (Would they have to stop condemning or talking about the "excessive one"? Would anyone lose an identity?)

- Can only one person in a family be smart? Hot-tempered? Happy? Sensitive? Worried? Depressed?

- Do you sometimes wish that your family would recognize that *you* are (smart, creative, sensitive, mature, capable, competent, responsible, athletic, musical, worried, etc.), too?

- What do you think happens when we mentally label our family members according to the roles we think they play? (Members aren't seen as complex individuals. They live up to their images. They feel they can't be or do otherwise. They believe they can't have the characteristic that someone else is noted for.)

4. Ask, "Would any of you like to change a role you play in your family?" Then ask the following:

   - What would you have to do to make the change?
   - Who would be affected?
   - Would your change cause other changes? If so, what other changes?
   - What could be a first step in making that important change?

5. For closure, ask someone to summarize the discussion, or ask volunteers to tell what they learned through the discussion, thought about in a new way, or felt. Thank them for their thoughtful and valuable contributions. Collect and dispose of the questionnaires.

family roles

Which family member(s) do you associate with the following roles?

leader	teacher of skills	"adult"
_____	_____	_____
planner	"child"	sensitive
_____	_____	_____
responsible	easy to raise	easily upset
_____	_____	_____
gets the most attention	difficult to raise	calm
_____	_____	_____
gets the least attention	social	hot-tempered
_____	_____	_____
playful	peacemaker	joker
_____	_____	_____
happy	nostalgic/sentimental about the past	sad
_____	_____	_____
emotional	instruction-giver	disciplinarian
_____	_____	_____
business manager	worrier	map-reader
_____	_____	_____
caretaker	angry	always comes up with new ideas
_____	_____	_____
rule-maker	not taken seriously	"pet"
_____	_____	_____
"wise one"	"smart one"	perfectionist
_____	_____	_____

Use these spaces to write in other roles that apply to your family:

_____   _____   _____

_____   _____   _____

Now go back and circle any role assignment that bothers you. You may circle more than one.

focus: family
personal space and privacy

background

The idea of "boundaries" is related to the focus of this session. Each of us is most healthy when we are clear about where we begin and end, and where others begin and end. When we are clear about who we are as separate individuals, we are not as likely to feel "sucked in" to others' problems and emotions and to feel responsible for their behavior. We are also more likely to be able to say "no" when we should, to set limits on our involvement even at school or work, and to protect ourselves from being used, abused, or used up by people and situations. That kind of psychological space may offer serenity even in the midst of family turmoil.

Having personal, private physical space at home might be a rare luxury for some students—perhaps even impossible. However, in homes where private physical space seems nonexistent, it may be even more important to speak of boundaries. Perhaps personal space is only a drawer of keepsakes, the top bunk, or a box under a bed containing personal writings. Whatever the size of the physical space, it is important to the person who claims it.

Privacy is usually a big issue for adolescents. It offers a chance to assert independence and uniqueness and to establish boundaries. It provides time and space to daydream, contemplate personal identity, and just be. Invading an adolescent's privacy—for example, by reading mail or journals, or examining closets or book bags—can cause great conflict and destroy trust. Knowing when it is appropriate to breach the boundaries of privacy and not to trust, such as when secrecy may involve dangerous behavior or substances, is always a difficult call. Parents must consider carefully questions like "What are my issues vs. my child's issues? What are clearly my parental responsibilities?" They should also look carefully at their own views of privacy and personal space. Perhaps the boundaries between them and their parents were unclear when they were growing up, and family members freely invaded one another's privacy. It may be time to change that habit while their adolescent is still at home. In fact, the adolescent might be able to initiate some new boundary-setting.

Suggestions #2 and #3 are appropriate for adolescents of any age; suggestions #4 and #5 are probably most appropriate for older adolescents and could form the basis for a separate session. Use your own judgment when deciding which suggestions to try with your group.

95

objectives

- Students think about their need for personal space.
- They become more aware of their family's attitudes about individual privacy and space.
- They see the importance of setting limits and establishing boundaries about time, space, belongings, and emotional involvement.

suggestions

1. Introduce the topic by talking about boundaries between people, using ideas from "Background." Ask group members if they have had trouble with privacy issues at home, either with parents or with siblings. Be aware that cultures and families vary regarding attitudes about personal space, and remember that differences should not be assessed as better or worse, using the dominant culture as the standard of "right." And be aware that adolescents are not always eager to talk about such differences, especially considering the need to fit in. There is also the possibility that someone can have private psychological space even when there is no physical space that is private. Acknowledge that *personal* space is important, particularly during adolescence.

2. Ask the group about private space at home with questions like these:

   - Are you able to have an area in your home that you feel is yours and no one else's?
   - Do you share space with a sibling or siblings?
   - If so, how successfully do you manage mutual respect for each other's space and belongings?
   - Do you have physical space that is supposed to be yours, but others invade it?
   - How do your parents treat your space?
   - How do you treat your space? Do you have special responsibilities for taking care of it?
   - How much do family members read your mail, look at school papers, or look through your belongings without your permission?
   - Does it bother you if they do? (There might be cultural differences here. You might consider discussing those differences further.)
   - Have you ever given your parent(s) reason not to trust what you have or do in your space? If so, would you be willing to share the circumstances?
   - Are there times when parents should invade a child's space? If so, when?
   - If there are problems with others not respecting your space, have you spoken to your family about that? (Affirm that as adolescents mature, these issues may become more and more significant.

Perhaps group members need to remind their parents of that reality. It might be helpful to speak of privacy before it becomes an even bigger issue, and before that concern is more likely to raise suspicion.)

3. Address the problems that group members have shared concerning invasion of space or lack of respect for belongings or personal life. Encourage group members to offer suggestions for dealing with these, based on their own experiences. Rehearse requests that could be made to family members, or role-play dialogues involving boundary-setting. Encourage I-statements ("I feel invaded when you look through my papers or clothes." "I have a right to privacy." "It bothers me when even my most personal things get tampered with").

4. Especially if your group is made up of older adolescents, and if time remains, introduce the idea of "emotional boundaries." However, be careful not to underestimate the ability of younger students to deal effectively with this issue. If you want to ask the following questions in a poll-taking manner, in order to find commonalities and move the discussion efficiently to suggestion #5, ask closed questions here, beginning with "Do" and "Are."

    ▶ How able are you *not* to be drawn into other family members' emotions? For example, if someone else has a bad day, can you avoid being drawn into his or her mood?

    ▶ How much do you get drawn into arguments with an unhappy parent or sibling?

    ▶ How much do you draw others into your unhappiness?

    ▶ How able are you to say to yourself, "No matter how much chaos/upheaval/stress they've got, I don't have to feel responsible for it or for doing something about it"?

    ▶ How much do you feel responsible for other family members' feelings and behavior?

    ▶ How much do you feel responsible for making the family "feel good"?

    ▶ How much do you feel that you are emotionally controlled, uncomfortably, by someone in the family?

    ▶ How much are you able to resist saying, "You *make* me feel...," and say instead, "I feel..."? (Explain that this is about "owning" your feelings and not claiming that others are responsible for them.)

    ▶ How much do you blame others for arguments you are part of at home?

    ▶ How much do you think emotional boundaries are a problem for you?

5. Rehearse some boundary-setting statements in the group that might be the start of clearer emotional boundaries. Call the group's attention to the use of "I."

    ▶ "Today I felt frustrated (sad, scared) when...." (Someone did something hurtful, harmful, irresponsible, or destructive.)

    ▶ "I can see that you're unhappy and upset, but I'm not going to get into an argument with you right now." (Someone who is sad or angry is trying to pick a fight with you.)

    ▶ "No, I didn't make you do that." (Someone just spilled something and blamed you.)

    ▶ "I realize that no one makes me do or feel anything. I have a choice about what I do and how I react." (You talk to yourself when you are tempted to blame someone else for what you did or how you reacted.)

    ▶ "I'm responsible for my own emotions, not theirs." (You talk to yourself because someone continually claims that you are responsible for the way he or she is feeling.)

    ▶ "I feel that you want me to take sides, but I'm not going to do that." (Someone is telling you about a conflict between two people you know well and is encouraging you to condemn one of them.)

    ▶ "I'm going to try to take better care of myself. It's so easy to make other people's problems mine, and I'm sure they don't really intend for me to do that. I'm not very good at knowing what my responsibility is and what isn't. It's easy to be drawn into other people's emotional situations, and that exhausts me sometimes." (In a quiet moment, you reflect on your life and decide to establish better boundaries between yourself and others.)

    Encourage group members to create and share statements that fit their situations.

6. For closure, ask one group member or a few to summarize what has been heard in the group.

focus: family
becoming separate

Having emotional comfort with family members helps a person to handle stressful situations. Resolving conflict among family members is, of course, desirable as one moves into adulthood, yet that process can be a long and bumpy journey, as parents and adolescents challenge and criticize each other. According to Murray Bowen, a significant systems-oriented theorist, children who are most entangled in family emotional conflict have the most difficulty separating from the family, even if they can't wait to leave and even if they cut themselves off from the family by moving away and not being in contact. Those who are not so involved in family conflict have less trouble becoming autonomous and carry less anxiety into adult life. Intense needs, fears, and anxieties that are related to family conflict can continue for decades, with impact on adult relationships.

Success in marriage is often related to the fact that the partners have healthily separated from their families, have their own identities, and have clear boundaries, a sense of competence, and autonomy. They are not as likely to feel responsible for others' emotions, to be overly involved in others' emotions, to rush to fix others' problems, or to have to pull away from emotional situations to protect themselves. If their important needs have been met, or if they have figured out ways to meet their needs themselves, they are not as likely to be overwhelmed by their own or others' needs—or to overwhelm their friends, spouse, or partner with their needs.

For many individuals in the United States, movement into adulthood has no clear "rite of passage." No ceremony or special process marks it, and therefore other "rites"—such as general risk-taking, substance use, and experimenting with lifestyles that contrast with those of the parents—become a means to separation. That transition is further complicated by prolonged financial dependency on parents, especially when college is in the picture. What at least the dominant culture sees as healthy "interdependent autonomy" may be long delayed and may therefore involve a long and complex journey.

reference

Bowen, M. "Theory in the practice of psychotherapy." In P. J. Guerin, Jr., ed., *Family Therapy: Theory and Practice* (New York: Gardner Press, 1976).

objectives

- Students gain insight into the often difficult process of finding a separate identity and effecting a healthy separation from parents.
- They learn about the part conflict can play in the separation process.

suggestions

1. Introduce the topic with some comments about how conflict is often part of the transition into adulthood, which involves separating from parents. This process can begin early and last a long time. Conflict may involve clothes, friends, decisions, curfew, car, homework, or any other area in an adolescent's life—and it may be major or minor, just irritating, greatly frustrating, and even heart-rending. Suggest to the group that what they see as their parents' "mistakes" and "stupidity" (as in, for example, "Their views are so *stupid!*") might even be doing them a favor by encouraging them to think as separate, competent individuals, not tempted to live at home as adults later! On the other hand, conflict that is not resolved as a person moves through adolescence into adulthood can interfere with separation, continuing to bind, entangle, and interfere with progress toward healthy interdependence/independence.

2. Proceed with questions like the following:

   - In what areas of your life are you becoming more and more independent and self-sufficient?
   - In what ways are you asserting yourself in order to let your family know you are a separate and unique person?
   - How are you taking care of yourself in new ways?
   - What decisions are you making on your own?
   - In what ways are you still dependent on your parent(s)?

3. Move into a discussion of conflict with questions like these:

   - What are some areas of current conflict between you and your parent(s)?
   - Which ones might still be issues 5–10 years from now?
   - What would it take to resolve those conflicts?
   - What effect is the conflict with your parent(s) having on your life and their lives?
   - Do you worry about the level of conflict you are experiencing now?
   - Does the level of conflict seem to fluctuate?
   - Are certain things causing particular conflict right now?
   - How soon do you think your situation will change?

Assure the group that nothing stays the same, including conflict. It can diminish or escalate as circumstances change.

4. Address the separation process more directly with these questions:

   ▶ What do you think your parent(s) are worrying about as you separate from them?

   ▶ What are your fears and worries as you begin to separate?

   ▶ How far away from your parent(s) do you think you will want to live as an adult?

   ▶ What might your mother or father have a difficult time with when you leave home?

   ▶ What would be an ideal relationship with your parent(s) when you are 20? When you are 35?

5. Invite group members to give examples of what they consider "healthy" and "unhealthy" separation from parents. You might mention that the *amount* of contact with parents is not the main concern regarding "healthy" and "unhealthy." A person can have frequent contact with parents and still be an independent adult. A person can be completely cut off from parents and still be connected to them in an emotionally unhealthy way—with intense, ongoing inner conflict. The ideal is a comfortable, mutually supportive adult relationship with one's parents. Some keys to achieving such a relationship are the following:

   ▶ feeling competent about making decisions independently

   ▶ taking responsibility for one's own life

   ▶ being able to resist involvement in "old" family conflict.

6. For closure, ask someone to summarize what they have heard the group say or what they have thought about or felt during the discussion. Ask these questions:

   ▶ Is "separation process" a good way to describe what you are going through? Or does that description seem inappropriate?

   ▶ What does the process feel like to you?

focus

relationships

focus: relationships

general background

Relationships contribute significantly to degree of satisfaction, feelings of self-worth, and balance in life. For some teens, positive and satisfying relationships seem to come easily. For others, relationships are hard both to establish and to sustain.

This series of sessions deals with several of the various relationships students are likely to have: with parents, with siblings, with teachers, with peers, and with romantic partners.

One kind of relationship might be the focus for a single session only, or it might be a sustained focus for more than one session. Or the relationship with parents, for example, might be the focus for one session, and other relationships might be discussed several sessions later. Certain groups might need to spend more time than others with a particular topic. Select discussion topics according to the needs of your group.

general objectives

- Students focus on various relationships in their lives and learn to articulate their feelings about them.
- They discover common concerns regarding relationships.
- They have opportunities to help each other with problem-solving about relationships.
- They ponder how various relationships contribute to feelings of self-worth, to goals, and to a sense of self.

focus: relationships
friendship

Friendship is an issue as individuals grow and mature. Not all teens want to discuss it, but all have likely thought about it a great deal, whether positively or negatively.

Friendships for young children are often formed because of proximity. A few years later, common interests play a part. Personality or shared backgrounds might be the key at a later age. Perhaps all through life, one person has only one close friend at a time, while another person always has many, with those varying in degree of closeness.

Some children and teens have difficulty making and/or keeping friends, and they struggle with loneliness. On the other hand, some seem to be content without much social involvement or close associations. Others have experienced pain and loss in friendships. Some have felt betrayal and loss of trust in friendships. Some have been sustained through uneven times by friends.

Experiences with friendship have an impact on whether a person ultimately feels social ease. A child learns social skills through friendship, including appropriate personal communication, conflict management, mutual support and assistance, and give-and-take about wishes and needs. Just as family environment contributes to the capacity to empathize and interact comfortably, so do experiences in friendship.

Students who have extremely high ability sometimes have difficulty finding "mind-mates"—not only for their unique interests, but also for their level of mental processing and sensitivity. Such uniqueness is often not valued in our society and may be seen as "weird." The loneliness that can result, especially when a student is in a school with few kindred spirits, can be painful. Discussion groups made up of just high-ability students offer opportunity to interact about social concerns with others who are their intellectual peers.

In this session, students can teach each other about friendship and about themselves as they share experiences and insights. Friendships might grow out of such discussion. Skills gained in articulating feelings and thoughts will be helpful all through life. Students who are at risk, whether "gifted at risk" or from somewhere else in the broad range of ability, can find safety in a discussion group dealing with this subject. If they have felt alienated or invisible in school, the group might help them to "be known" in a positive way.

objectives

- Students examine feelings and share concerns about friendship.
- They articulate what they have learned through friendships.
- They share friendship experiences.
- They find affirmation for their own uniqueness and gain confidence in themselves as being worthy of friendship.

suggestions

1. Ask the students to define "friendship." Encourage several to contribute to this introduction of the topic. Be alert to the words they use, and follow up with questions about their choice of descriptors.

2. Hand out copies of "Friendship" (page 108) and ask the students to fill out the questionnaire with brief responses, anonymously. Use the questionnaire to generate discussion. Or give each student a copy of the questionnaire and make it an oral exercise only, moving down the list of questions, choosing at random or asking the students which questions they would like to discuss. Tell them that they can omit or "pass" on any questions they don't wish to answer. Assess the trust level in the group carefully as you choose which questions to pursue for discussion. If you don't insist on a response from everyone for each question, you will probably be able to use all of the questions.

3. Be aware that some students may not have friends to describe. You might ask those in the group who make friends easily to articulate what they like and look for in a friend. Even if they have never considered that they have skills for friendship, ask some to share how they would teach others to make friends, using their responses for question #16 from the "Friendship" handout.

4. Ask the group, "What are some common struggles in friendship at your age?" Discuss what can make it difficult to keep friendships going. (Suggest the following, if the students don't mention them: changing interests, moving, new activities, being chosen or not chosen for participation in something, personality differences, moodiness, or dating outside a friendship group.)

5. Focus on what each person in the group can offer a friendship. They can make statements about themselves, or they can comment about the assets of others in the group.

6. Discuss how people differ in their need for many friends. Affirm those in the group who are not as socially oriented as others—perhaps because they are more self-sufficient, or perhaps because they prefer to be close to only one person or a few.

7. Focus on sharing confidences by asking questions like these:

   ▶ If someone chooses you to confide in, what message does that send to you? (Is that a compliment?)

   ▶ If you choose a particular person to confide in, what message does that send to him or her? (That he or she is respected? Trusted? A good listener?)

   ▶ What do you expect from people you confide in? (That they just listen? Respect your confidentiality? Offer advice?)

8. For closure, invite a few to share how they felt during the discussion— at ease, thoughtful, uncomfortable, inspired, sad, relaxed, grateful? Be aware that group members who are lonely may not have found the discussion to be uplifting. Leave enough time to be able to hear and validate those feelings, but don't press anyone to comment. If nothing seems to need discussion, and time remains, ask the group what they found they had in common. Encourage them to say at least "Hi" when they see each other in the future, no matter whether they are in the same friendship group or not. Commend them for what they did well. Collect and dispose of the questionnaires.

friendship

1. How have your friendships changed over the past year or two?
   _____

2. What do you value in your best friend(s)?
   _____

3. What do your friends value in you?
   _____

4. Is it easy for you to make friends? Yes ☐ No ☐
   If not, what seems to make it difficult?
   _____

5. Is it easy for you to keep friendships going? Yes ☐ No ☐
   If not, what seems to cause problems?
   _____

6. Do you have friends of different ages? Yes ☐ No ☐

7. What are some things you and your friends have in common?
   _____

8. What are some things you don't have in common with your friends?
   _____

9. What makes friendships different for people your age than for people a
   few years younger than you?
   _____

10. What do you think makes adult friendships different from friendships at your age?
    _____

11. Do you have some friends your parents don't approve of? Yes ☐ No ☐
    If so, what kinds of problems does that cause for you?
    _____

12. What have you learned through friendships?
    _____

13. Have you ever lost a friend because one of you moved away? Yes ☐ No ☐
    If you have, was it difficult to adjust to that loss? Yes ☐ No ☐

14. Have you ever felt rejected by a friend? Yes ☐ No ☐
    If you have, how did you help yourself handle the rejection?
    _____
    Do you still think about it? Yes ☐ No ☐

15. Do you quickly develop close friendships, or are you hesitant to become involved in a
    close friendship? _____

16. What advice would you give to someone who has difficulty making friends?
    _____

focus: relationships
small talk and social graces

background

Social ease comes from experience—and sometimes from courage and conscious effort to learn social skills. Most adolescents do not readily admit to being uncomfortable socially, but most do worry about what to do or say on occasion. Some parents take the time to teach specific skills. Others do not, and children are left to learn by observation and, often, through trial-and-error. This session gives students a chance to talk honestly about what they feel inept at and to practice some skills.

When they have little opportunity to practice formal behavior, they may feel uncomfortable whenever they sense that something proper is in order. This session encourages students to discuss such situations. Students who have a poor fit with "the system" might have little faith that conversation at school, for instance, could ever be comfortable and smooth for them. Discussion might be able to boost their confidence.

If yours is a group with high ability, make the observation that many people with high intellect are so fearful of clichés and "sounding stupid" that they have trouble initiating conversations, commenting on the weather, or making people feel at ease—and some have trouble sustaining conversations because they are overly concerned about both "saying things right" and saying the right things. Obviously, other students can have the same problems. No matter whether group members are all-American superstars or the most uninvolved or awkward teens in school, they will appreciate the concern for their social ease.

objectives

- Students learn and practice important skills for social ease.
- They appreciate the need for social graces in and outside of school.

suggestions

1. Introduce the topic by exploring with the group what is difficult for them socially. Ask questions like these, letting nods suffice for the last three closed questions, since that is enough to let group members know that others share their concerns:

    ❯ What social situations are uncomfortable for people your age?

109

> ▶ Do you have trouble with small talk? With introductions? With strangers? With formal situations?

> ▶ Do you have trouble starting conversations?

> ▶ Are you uncomfortable in groups?

Ask for examples of social situations where they feel uncomfortable.

2. Invite the group members to share suggestions for behavior in the following situations:

funerals	dances
weddings	job interviews
visiting someone in a hospital	visiting someone else's place of worship
being introduced to your parents' friends	eating a meal with a friend's family
meeting new people your own age	receiving a gift
formal concerts where classical music is played	staying overnight at a friend's house
music events geared to your age group	needing to thank a host family for an overnight visit
eating at a nice restaurant	meeting your girlfriend's/boyfriend's parents

For each situation, ask:

> ▶ If you have ever been in this situation, what have you felt uncomfortable about?

> ▶ What have you learned that has made this type of situation easier for you?

3. Offer the students a chance to practice various skills. Set up role-playing situations to practice the following:

> ▶ a firm handshake, and some etiquette surrounding that action

> ▶ introducing a friend, parents, a teacher

> ▶ starting a conversation with a stranger

> ▶ starting a conversation with someone on the way out of class

> ▶ asking someone if it's all right to eat lunch with him or her

> ▶ striking up a conversation with a seat partner on a bus, a plane, the subway, at a bus stop, at the swimming pool, at a recreation center

> ▶ responding to someone who makes a comment about the weather

▶ asking questions of someone as a way of showing interest (beginning with "Do you live around here?" or "Are you new here?" or "What do you think of this class?" or "Do you often come here?" and following that idea with interested comments and further questions).

4. For closure, have the group pair off. Invite them to shake hands firmly (without pumping the arm), and, while holding the other person's hand solidly, to express appreciation for something ("I really appreciate what you say in our group." "I'm glad you're in our group." "I've really appreciated getting to know you"). If necessary, model this interaction for the students. Encourage them not to worry about sounding clichéd. Explain that sometimes a plain, simple, direct comment is best. Then have them change partners and wish each other well in life ("I hope you have a good life"), again with a handshake.

Before they leave, ask them how the activity felt. Ask questions like these:

▶ Was it comfortable for you?

▶ Was the hand-shaking helpful, or did it make the experience less comfortable for you?

▶ Was it good to connect physically?

▶ How did it feel to say something plain, simple, and direct?

▶ Did it help to know in advance that this would be all right?

focus: relationships
gossip

There is usually no shortage of gossip among adolescents—in school and elsewhere. Gossip is no stranger to many age groups, of course. It has power, and it can hurt, control, backfire, boomerang, become more and more distorted, and detract from both the gossiper and the person who is gossiped about. This topic should generate much discussion.

objectives

- Students consider the role gossip plays in adolescent conversation.
- They consider how gossip affects their lives and the lives of others.
- They consider how much they participate in gossip themselves.

important

With all of the questions, remember that it is important not to pass judgment or to moralize. Just let group members express their feelings, experiences, and opinions, and you will probably be inspired by their conclusions. The most important messages will be in their own comments.

suggestions

1. Ask the group to define "gossip." Invite them to offer opinions as to whether it is a positive or negative force in society generally and in their lives. Steer the discussion toward gossip as related to relationships and as something that contributes to conversation.

2. Invite discussion about their experiences with gossip. Ask questions like these, and encourage group members to elaborate when appropriate—discreetly, of course:

   ▶ Have you ever been hurt by gossip?

   ▶ Have you ever known of someone else being hurt by gossip?

   ▶ Have you ever passed along some gossip and then found out it wasn't true? What, if anything, did you do about it?

   ▶ Do you think you are a gossip?

   ▶ Do your peers think of you as a gossip?

   ▶ Do you knowingly add spice to gossip when passing it on?

▶ Does everyone gossip to some extent?

▶ Who do you think gossips more—males or females? (Is gossip perhaps the female counterpart to male aggression? Is it more difficult to know who the aggressor is when gossip is the weapon, than when the first strike is shoving or hitting? Is one type of weapon more cruel than the other? Do males, in fact, gossip as much as females? There is plenty to discuss here.)

▶ Do you know someone who refuses to gossip, or who seems not to be excited by it?

▶ Can gossip be an addiction?

▶ Are you able *not* to pass gossip along when you have heard something interesting?

▶ How do you usually respond to an invitation to hear some gossip?

▶ Have you ever told someone that you didn't want to hear his or her gossip?

▶ Is your family "into gossip"?

▶ Is your group of friends "into gossip"?

▶ What do gossips get out of gossiping? (A sense of power? A feeling of belonging? A chance to hurt someone?)

▶ How would you rank these in importance in your social world?

   ▪ talking about things (possessions, purchases, clothing, houses, etc.)

   ▪ talking about people (gossip, who is going with whom, deaths and divorces, movie and music stars, people in the news, etc.)

   ▪ talking about ideas (thoughts about life, politics, meaning, creative ways to do things, insights about self and others, etc.)

▶ How would you rank the above in quality of conversation?

3. For closure, ask someone to summarize the session. Ask the group if the discussion raised their awareness of the power of gossip and what it is used for. Did it raise their awareness about themselves? What feelings did it provoke?

focus: relationships
being interesting

background

Adolescents are sometimes concerned that they are not interesting, or that someday they will lose a relationship because they are no longer interesting. They believe they have seen it happen in their lives—perhaps in their families. Even while they are in school, most worry about being interesting in connection with social acceptance and popularity. To enhance their appeal, they buy the right clothes, make sure they can talk about the right things, develop strong likes and dislikes to be shared in conversation, and work hard to become good at something. But they still might not be sure they are interesting. Others, of course, may choose not to worry about how they appear or to compete for that kind of "interesting." Still others may believe they *cannot* compete.

Some may not have to work at being interesting. They just *are*—in the eyes of their peers. For some of them, being interesting might mean being popular. For others, it might mean that they are seen as colorful, dramatic, mysterious, or complex. Whatever the label means, even kindergartners can judge who is interesting—and appealing.

This topic is pertinent to all students, for all are developing identity, and all want to be noticed—to some degree, at least. They want to know if they are interesting, whether they are the most successful students in school, the most shy, or the ones who are most often in trouble. This can be a relaxing, light discussion. The group might need that. Enjoy it.

objectives

- Students feel affirmed for their uniquenesses.
- They learn that they may differ in their views about what is interesting.

suggestions

1. Introduce the topic by asking the group what makes people interesting. They might consider their own age group first, and then adults. If a chalkboard is available, make a list of their criteria.

2. Have the group members name some interesting peers—and then some interesting adults—and support their nominations with a statement or two.

114

3. Ask them if "being interesting" is a concern for them. Introduce the idea that we are all more interesting than we think we are. There are probably many, many experiences, situations, relatives, accidents, struggles, traumas, moments, and neighborhood memories that we haven't thought about for a long time, but which, if they were known, would make us come to life for someone. However, we also need to remember that just responding to whatever is around us, and showing that we are interested in whoever we are with, is interesting enough to make us good company and pleasant to be around.

4. Ask the students to make a list on paper of 5–10 interesting things about themselves—things that few group members, if any, know. (Maybe they have a significant scar, a history of a dozen moves, a pilot's license, a musical talent not displayed in school, a position in their religious organization, ten siblings, an eccentric relative, a penny collection, a weird recurring dream, an attic bedroom, a unique part-time job, a strange allergy, a fascination for off-beat movies, a weakness for chocolate, or....?)

   Have each person share his or her list with a partner, who will ask for elaboration on just one of the items from the list. Re-form the group and have each person tell what he or she learned about his or her interesting partner. They can report on more than one of the 5–10 items, or concentrate on the one that was elaborated on.

5. For closure, affirm them as interesting persons. Let them know that bits of history and habits, and quirks of personality, do make people interesting. In relationships, sharing the homey personal side, the idiosyncrasies, and the stories makes people real and human—and interesting. When people say "Yes!" to who they are, and where they have been, *in addition* to showing interest in those they are with, they are likely to be easy and fun to be around. Ask the group for comments about how it felt to share their interesting details. Was it comfortable, encouraging, affirming, fun?

focus: relationships
conformity

- Students recognize that conformity is part of the adolescent social world, as well as the academic world.

- They examine how they are responding to the pressures to conform and not to conform, and they consider possible sources of these pressures.

- They consider the price of both conformity and nonconformity and the value of responsibly challenging the pressure to conform.

1. Begin by asking the group how much they generally conform to the majority in the following situations. Then ask them how much they conform to a minority. In either case, it might be with clothing style, behavior, social activity, attitude, music tastes, food or drink choices, or lifestyle. Their level of conformity might differ, depending on their context.

socially at school	at work
academically at school	socially outside of school
at home	

2. Ask them how they feel they show their uniqueness in the above situations. Then pursue these strands:

   - What encourages you to conform?

   - What encourages you not to conform?

   - Is it easier or harder to resist conformity when you are with your friends?

   - Who sets the standards in each of the worlds mentioned in the first question—school, work, outside of school, home?

   - Is there a right way to behave in each of these worlds?

   - When might conformity be bad? (Expect a variety of answers and opinions, including when the pressure is on for behavior that is dangerous to ourselves or others, or to public safety or property.)

   - When might conformity be good? (When it is in someone's best interests? When it is necessary for survival? When it is "smart"?)

> What price might we pay for conformity? (Loss of individuality? Anger at ourselves for bowing to pressure? Loss of creativity? Loss of valuable ideas? Personal harm, if the conformity means exposing ourselves to danger?)

> What price might we pay for nonconformity? (Losing out on what can be gained from "the system"? Loss of opportunity? Disruption and hassle? Loneliness? Ostracism? Abuse? Ridicule?)

> Are you a better person if you conform? If you don't conform?

> How do you feel about conformists generally? About nonconformists?

> Are you mostly a conformist or mostly a nonconformist?

> How do you feel about your level of conformity or nonconformity?

> What does your family value most, conformity or nonconformity?

3. If there is time, and if your group likes to move into the abstract, brainstorm nonconforming behaviors and ideas that have made big and small changes in society by moving society away from the way things had "always" been done. Ask them for their ideas first. Then offer these:

nose rings and other body piercings	organ transplants
fast food	mixing musical genres (Christian/rock; country/pop)
civil rights activism	airplane flight
feminism	movies on videotape available to the public
mixing animation with live actors in film	shopping malls
drive-in movies	telemarketing
the three-point shot in basketball	infomercials
the theory of relativity	laptop computers
drive-through banking	E-mail

4. For closure, invite the students to express some of the feelings and thoughts they had during the session. Ask questions like these:

> Did you think of conformity and nonconformity in new ways? In what new ways?

> Did the way you see yourself change during the course of the discussion? If so, how?

> How did you feel during the discussion—uneasy, proud, comfortable?

117

focus: relationships with parents

objectives

- Students learn that parent-child struggles are common in their age group and are relatively normal.
- They examine their relationship with their parents.
- They learn to articulate some of the complexities in their relationship with their parents.
- They explore the idea that parenting styles differ.
- They gain some understanding of both themselves and their parents.

important

For discussion purposes, "parents" can refer to biological and/or adoptive parents, step-parents, foster parents, guardians, or other significant caretaking adults. If a parent is no longer living, even if the relationship was brief, that relationship might still be significant here. The same may be true for a former step-parent or foster parent.

1. If group members have not already described their various family situations in the Focus: Family sessions, you might have them briefly describe the family they live with. Some, of course, are in situations involving blended families, current or past step-parents, absent parents, deceased parents, "distant" parents, single parents, adoptive parents, or unknown parents. Remind them at the outset that the "typical" family of the past may no longer be typical at all. Encourage them to consider all such parent relationships as important and worthy of discussion. All such relationships have an impact on a young life.

2. Hand out copies of "Relationships with Parents" (page 121) and ask the students to fill out the questionnaire with brief responses, anonymously. Use the questionnaire to generate discussion. Or simply give each student a copy of the questionnaire to use as a reference during the discussion. You might take one question at a time and go quickly around the group for brief answers. As always, the value is in raised awareness and experience in expressing concerns.

3. Introduce the idea of "parenting style." Use the following questions to explore this. Beware of overtly passing judgment on responses, even though biases and values are implicit in several of the questions. The questions for this suggestion and Suggestion #4 talk in terms of "parents," but not all group members will have two parents. Those who do might have very different relationships with each parent. Steer the direction accordingly, and invite group members to consider their parents individually when framing their responses to the questions.

   ▶ How unified are your parents? For example, if they both live with you, do they agree on rules about discipline and support, and not disagree in front of you and your siblings? Or, if they don't live together, do they agree on how you should be treated?

   ▶ How clear are their guidelines?

   ▶ How patient are your parents? How casual? Formal? Rule-oriented? Consistent?

   ▶ When you do something you shouldn't do or break a family rule, is punishment immediate? Harsh? Fair? Appropriate?

   ▶ How much do your parents "preach" or "lecture"? Allow you to learn from your mistakes? Give advice?

   ▶ How much independence do they give you? How much do they allow you to make decisions?

   ▶ How protective are they? How affectionate are they toward you?

   ▶ How seriously do they take parenting?

   ▶ Which of them leads—in various areas of family life?

   ▶ How do they divide their parenting responsibilities?

4. Ask these questions:

   ▶ Have you been easy for your parents to raise?

   ▶ Have your parents been easy to have as parents? (Acknowledge that some adolescents might even feel that they have had to "raise their parents"!)

   ▶ What kinds of feelings do you have when you think about, or talk about, your parents? (They might use "feeling" words like "grateful," "angry," "frustrated," "happy," "sad," "lucky," "depressed," "nostalgic," "secure," or "guilty." Remind them that it is good to practice speaking at a feelings level—to enhance relationships and to learn how to assess feelings and behavior accurately.)

   ▶ What are the major "jobs" of parents, in your opinion?

   ▶ Which of these "jobs" have your parents done well?

5. If time permits, invite the group to consider how their relationships with parents and step-parents have contributed to the following:

their personal goals	their school success
their view of life	other relationships
their understanding of what "family" is	their feelings of self-worth

6. For closure, summarize—or have a student summarize—what some of the most significant discussion ideas have been during this session. The relationship with each parent is significant in forming the self. There is value in discussing these relationships, which are always complex and often troublesome, especially during adolescence. Thank the group for their honesty and thoughtfulness and for helping the group to understand better the complexities of relationships with parents. Collect and dispose of the questionnaires.

relationships with parents

Use your own judgment about how to answer these questions if you don't live with one or both parents; if you live with a step-parent, but have contact with the parent not living with you; if you live with foster parents, adoptive parents, or a guardian; or if a parent is no longer living. Feel free to omit some questions or to think about how your parent was when he or she was with you.

1. Describe the relationship you have with your mother. _____
   _____

2. Describe the relationship you have with your father. _____
   _____

3. How are these relationships different from the way they were two years ago? _____
   _____
   Five years ago? _____
   Ten years ago? _____

4. What specific problems, if any, interfere with your having a good relationship with your parents?
   _____

5. Which parent are you closest to? _____

6. Which parent do you feel you resemble the most physically? _____
   Emotionally? _____

7. Is one or both of your parents absent? Ill? No longer living? Not around much? _____
   _____
   If so, how have you coped with that? _____
   _____

8. How do your parents cope with stress and frustrations? _____
   _____
   With child-rearing? _____

9. How are they coping with your getting older? _____
   _____

10. How do they respond when you are ill? _____
    When you are in trouble? _____

11. What do you respect most about your parents? _____

12. What have your parents done well in life? (Your answer can relate to any area of life.)
    _____

13. What are the most important things your parents have taught you? _____
    _____

14. Write five words that come to mind when you think "Dad" or "Father." _____
    _____

15. Write five words that come to mind when you think "Mom" or "Mother." _____
    _____

focus: relationships with siblings

objectives

- Students gain insight into their relationships with brothers and sisters.
- They gain skills in articulating feelings and concerns about their family context.
- They consider how family conflict helps to form personal identity.

suggestions

1. Introduce the focus, and then ask each group member to do the following:
   - give the names and ages of their siblings and step-siblings (even if this was done in a previous session)
   - give a brief description, perhaps 2 or 3 adjectives, for each
   - explain what kind of relationship they have with each
   - (if a sibling no longer lives at home, has died, or is at home only part of the time) describe what kind of relationship they once had and whether it has changed.

2. Move the discussion in the direction of conflict with these questions:
   - Do you have old, ongoing conflicts with siblings?
   - Has there been more, or less, conflict in recent years?
   - How close do you feel to each sibling, on a scale of 1–10, with 10 being very close?
   - How much conflict do you feel with each sibling, on a scale of 1–10, with 10 being a lot of conflict?
   - What kinds of conflicts have you had with your siblings? Be specific.

Sharing concerns offers opportunities for problem-solving and learning from others' successful problem-solving. Group members might mention conflict areas such as these in answer to the last question above:

competition

jealousy

criticism

favoritism

age differences

personality differences

guilt

different interests

gender issues

needing a separate identity from each other

competition for parental approval

personal space

3. Move the discussion in a direction that offers a chance for group members to speak positively about their siblings. Ask the following questions:

▶ How much support and encouragement do you feel from your siblings?

▶ Do you feel grateful to them for anything/something? What, for example?

▶ Do you worry a lot about a sibling? Why?

▶ Do you believe that sibling relationships can change dramatically over time? Or do they not change?

4. Offer the idea that children strive for a separate identity in the family, different from their siblings', and seek attention from parents in various ways. Ask these questions:

▶ What separate identity do you have in your family? What are you known for in your family?

▶ Has it been difficult for you to gain a separate identity? Why or why not?

▶ Do you feel you have little or a lot of identity in your family?

▶ Do you think you have reacted *against* someone in creating your identity?

▶ How do family members usually describe you to others?

▶ Have you felt labeled by how they describe you? If so, how accurate is the label? Do you enjoy the label? Do you feel you have to live up to the label?

▶ Have you felt overshadowed by anyone in your family? If so, explain.

▶ Do you feel you have had *too much* attention? More than your siblings?

▶ How do you feel around each of your siblings? (Confident? Unconfident? Superior? Inferior?)

▶ Do you think that each child in your family feels a sense of important personal space and place?

5. For closure, ask for a volunteer to summarize the discussion. Or ask for various group members' impressions. Do most students seem to have smooth relationships with siblings, or do most have relationships with a lot of conflict? How did they feel during the discussion? Encourage them to use "feeling" words—like "comfortable," "uncomfortable," "sad," "happy," "uneasy," "guilty," "pleased," "proud," "grateful," "irritated."

   This might also be a good time to ask them how they are feeling about their group at this stage in their development as a group—especially if this and recent discussions have gone well, and if they have been meeting long enough to develop a good comfort level with each other.

focus: relationships with teachers

background

Most students are probably not aware of how "human" teachers really are. They may not realize that teachers do become concerned when students are ill or are in difficult situations; that teachers are often hesitant to ask personal questions; that teachers sometimes wonder how to express concern adequately or acceptably to students; and that teachers do see *individuals* in their classes each day, but numbers and time constraints often make it difficult to make conversation, express concern, or connect one-on-one.

Teachers have their own lives, and they should have clear boundaries between school and family in order to give each its due energy and attention. However, part of what makes teaching satisfying and rewarding is having healthy and comfortable teacher-student relationships. Such relationships probably help to sustain coaches and extracurricular advisors during their great time commitment to activities. Nevertheless, it is important that teachers remain *teachers* in student-teacher relationships. They are not peers of students, and they have special ethical responsibilities. Teacher-student relationships always have a power imbalance, for example, and there is a fine line between support/advice and interference/coercion/manipulation. Teachers who need to be close to students—for their own benefit, not the students'—may cross another fine line. And there is a great difference between teachers confiding in students and students confiding in teachers. Teachers can be of most help to students when they are *teachers first,* with all the complex dimensions of that position.

Some teachers, of course, are shy, just as some students are. Some teachers are very private people, just as some students are. Some teachers communicate easily with students outside of class, just as some students can with teachers. Each teacher and each student probably has unique wishes about communication with the other.

Teachers are major players in the lives of adolescents. Good teacher-student communication can contribute to crucial advocacy and support and may enhance motivation in the classroom.

objectives

- Students learn that attitudes about relationships with teachers vary within the group.
- They articulate their thoughts and feelings concerning relationships with teachers.
- They explore the advantages of having a good relationship with a teacher.

suggestions

1. If you are a teacher or counselor, introduce the topic by sharing your own thoughts about relationships with students. Do you consciously maintain clear boundaries between yourself and students, and between their lives and yours, even as you become an important teacher/counselor/friend? Have you ever become too close to a student? Then ask the group questions like these:

   ❱ Have you ever had a teacher or counselor who was a "teacher-friend"? (Suggest that a teacher-friend can be a special kind of friend and valuable ally—an adult to talk with, to trust, and to seek guidance from. A teacher-friend can be *most* helpful when the emphasis stays on "teacher," just as parent-friends are best when they are *parents* first. Whereas peer-friends are equal in sharing confidences, for example, adult-friends may be most helpful in being *un*equal and able to offer adult wisdom and support.)

   ❱ Was that relationship unique, or was it like any other friendship?

   ❱ Was that friendship different from friendships you have with other adults?

   You might want to mention the idea of professional boundaries. See "Background" for ideas.

2. Hand out copies of "Relationships with Teachers" (page 128) and ask the students to fill out the questionnaire with brief responses, anonymously. Use the questionnaire to generate discussion. Or make it an oral exercise only, with the students using the questionnaire as a visual reference during the discussion.

3. Ask the group these questions:

   ❱ What are some possible advantages of having a good, comfortable relationship with a teacher?

   ❱ Have you ever needed/asked a teacher to speak on your behalf to other teachers when you were having a problem in school?

   ❱ Have you ever known a teacher well enough to trust him or her with personal information?

   ❱ Has a teacher ever counseled you? How was that experience?

   ❱ How can students build a good teacher-student relationship?

▶ How might a teacher benefit from having a comfortable, communicative relationship with a student? With students in general?

4. Invite the group to problem-solve:

▶ Is there a teacher you aren't getting along with this year?

▶ How might improving the relationship benefit you?

▶ What could you do to change the relationship, so that it wouldn't be strained? (Ask for help; make eye contact; make small talk; answer questions in class; recognize that teachers need warmth and support, just like anyone else; arrange to speak individually with the teacher about the relationship.)

▶ Do you think parents or counselors should ever intervene to try to improve a relationship between a student and a teacher? (Suggest that it is probably best for the student to try to take care of the situation with the teacher first, alone, perhaps after guidance from parents or a counselor. If that attempt is unproductive, then someone else might be asked to serve as an objective third party in conflict resolution or to advocate directly.)

5. To prepare for closure, ask these questions:

▶ What do you need from teachers generally?

▶ What do you definitely *not* want from teachers?

6. For closure, ask someone to summarize what has been shared and/or learned during this discussion. Compliment the students on their ability to articulate thoughts and feelings. Collect and dispose of the questionnaires.

relationships with teachers

1. What kinds of relationships do you have with your various teachers? _____
   _____

2. In the past five years, have your relationships with teachers generally become closer and more
   comfortable, or more distant and less comfortable? _____
   _____

3. Name one teacher, present or past, who is/was a great teacher for you: _____
   What makes/made him or her so significant in your life? _____
   _____

4. What teaching style(s) do you like best? Circle one or more:

structured	little personal interaction with students
unstructured	using a lot of worksheets
highly organized	showing information visually
very flexible	great variety in each class period
few rules	giving information by speaking
many rules	giving information by having activities
clear guidelines	using a lot of technology
personal warmth	

   Do your choices here fit the great teacher you named in #3? Yes ☐ No ☐

5. Do you like to have teachers know you well personally? Yes ☐ No ☐

6. What kind of information do you like teachers to know about you? _____
   _____

   What kind of information do you *not* want to teachers to know about you? _____
   _____

7. If you were having a very difficult time in your personal life, would you want your teachers to be
   aware of that? Yes ☐ No ☐
   Why or why not? _____

8. How do you know when a teacher likes and enjoys you as a student? _____
   _____

   Do most teachers seem to like you? Yes ☐ No ☐

9. How do you let teachers know that you approve of their teaching? _____
   _____

focus: relationships
male and female

background

Sexuality involves much more than just having sex, of course. It is how we are distinguished, male and female—how we behave in response to physical sensations, how we interact in social relationships, and how we notice the responses of others. People vary in how they define what behaviors are appropriate for each gender. Opinions differ about how a male should "be male" and how a female should "be female"—within and among cultures, families, and groups of friends and colleagues. Adolescents, already struggling with identity issues, may have reason to be confused in regard to gender expectations, behavior, and sexual feelings.

This session introduces a series of sessions on gender relations. Suggestion #2 offers a chance for adolescents to find out what their peers think, for each gender to find out what the other gender thinks, and for you to learn about their views and concerns. That activity usually generates enough interaction to fill a session. Suggestion #3 might be considered as a follow-up session in itself, especially if a film is used. Looking at ads can be an effective second half of an introductory session on gender relations.

Students usually appreciate having a safe place, with an attentive adult listener, to discuss these important matters. As with all other sessions, it is important to listen and not preach. However, it is appropriate for you to give opinions carefully and sensitively if the students ask for them or seem to be looking for guidance.

important

You will need to do some advance preparation for Suggestion #3 in this session. If you plan to show a film or videotape concerning media messages about sexuality, check with your media center or library for ideas. Two videos appropriate for older students are *Killing Us Softly* and *Still Killing Us Softly,* which explore how women are portrayed in advertisements. Contact Cambridge Documentary Films, Lordly and Dame, Inc., 51 Church Street, Boston, MA 02116. If you plan to have the group analyze advertisements, make an assignment at the end of the previous session for students to bring in five ads that prominently feature females (or parts of females), males (or parts of males), or both males and females.

objectives

- Students consider their gender identity.
- They think about cultural attitudes regarding being male and female.
- They find comfort in the fact that their peers also have anxieties and confusion about sexuality.

suggestions

1. Invite the group to think of someone they find attractive. Then ask, "What is it about that person that you find especially appealing?"

2. Have group members make lists on the chalkboard of "what makes males male" and "what makes females female." Have the males make lists for both males and females, and have the females also make two lists. Then ask a spokesperson for each group to report.

   This activity usually provokes a wide range of behaviors, from silliness to arguing to quiet pondering, but it will also provoke serious thinking. The students undoubtedly will consider physical attributes at the outset, but very quickly they will probably list emotional, expressive, and other behavioral characteristics. At times they may find it difficult to assign specific qualities or characteristics to specific genders. Ask questions like these when they are done:

   ▶ Is being gentle, nurturing, and emotional only "female"?

   ▶ Is being assertive and strong only "male"?

   ▶ How much are you a mixture of all of these traits?

   ▶ (If someone insists on clear distinctions:) How do you feel about those distinctions? Are you more comfortable when there are clear distinctions?

   ▶ Who tells us that there have to be a clear distinctions?

   ▶ What are some mysteries you wish you knew more about in regard to the other gender?

   Reassure the group that probably most of us struggle or are uncomfortable at times about how we feel and act, because we wonder how we fit in with society's expectations of what males and females should be and do.

3. Show and discuss a videotape or film concerning media messages about sexuality. Or show and analyze the advertisements students brought to the group, focusing on gender roles and stereotypes, sexuality, and subtle messages. Ask these questions:

   ▶ What impact do messages in advertising have on relationships?

   ▶ How much are female and male bodies used to sell products?

   ▶ How might the way males and females are portrayed in ads be related to the way people behave on dates, in marriage, at work?

   ▶ Do you think that media images like these contribute to narrow gender expectations, sexual harassment, abuse, and even violence? Explain.

4. For closure, ask the group if this was a comfortable topic to discuss. Was it a new experience—to discuss sexuality in a group? Assure them that adolescence is a time when sexuality is a significant concern. Confusing thoughts are quite normal. Sexuality will probably continue to be an interesting topic for them.

focus: relationships
they're going out now

background

This session acknowledges that there is great concern during adolescence and young adulthood about relationships which involve "going out." There are concerns about how to behave, how to attract, what a potential date finds appealing, how assertive to be, what to say, how to be honest and real, what friends think, how to kiss someone, how to give attention to friends when absorbed in a dating relationship, and how to be comfortable when going out with someone. Then there are concerns about sex, pregnancy, sexually transmitted diseases, and date rape. Unfortunately, it is often difficult for adults and adolescents to discuss sexual matters together, which means that young people are often less informed than either they or the adults believe they are, and they have to depend on peers or the media for information—or misinformation.

Note: Toward the beginning of this session, you might want to ask your group members what words they use when they talk about relationships. "Going out," "going together," "dating," "seeing each other," "hanging out together"—what do they call it when two people are in a romantic relationship? During the session, try to use the language with which the students seem most comfortable.

important

In most settings, the focus of this session will probably be on heterosexual relationships. However, just because the majority of adolescents go out with persons of the opposite gender does not mean that we can or should ignore those who are attracted to their own gender.

It is not just those who have concluded that they are gay, lesbian, or bisexual who wonder what that means in a society that generally finds homosexual relationships unsettling. Words like "dyke," "fag," "lezzie," "fairy," and "queer-bait" are tossed around freely and negatively in schools today, reflecting the confusion, doubt, and self-consciousness about feelings that are typical of adolescence. Many adolescents, in fact, are targets at

132

some point as they form close same-gender friendships, pursue activities and careers considered nontraditional for their gender, and/or develop mannerisms that leave them vulnerable to name-calling. And the names resonate, because adolescence means searching for identity, which means confusion, doubt, and experimentation about many aspects of the self. Because of their fears, and because of the responses of others, some teens may run away or become suicidal. Lack of support and of open, honest discussion at home and at school undoubtedly contribute to their feeling alienated and desperate enough to want to put themselves at risk, and even to take their own lives.

Keeping in mind the constraints of your setting, and carefully considering the level of trust and comfort within your group, you might consider conducting a matter-of-fact discussion about same-gender relationships and partnerships, either as part of this session or as a separate session. If you feel uncomfortable or uncertain about how to do this, you might talk first with a school counselor or other adult professional who works with gay, lesbian, and bisexual teens.

Be aware that few, if any, gay, lesbian, or bisexual teens are likely to be open about their orientation. As a facilitator, you might therefore simply acknowledge that there may be teens in your setting who cannot relate to a discussion of heterosexual relationships. If group members appear to want to pursue that direction, encourage them to express their thoughts, feelings, and concerns. Ask them, 'What do you know about same-gender relationships?" Be prepared with information yourself that might refute myths and challenge prejudices. Explain that it is quite normal during adolescence to wonder about complex sexual feelings that may, in fact, be directed toward persons of the same gender. Close, intense friendships with people of the same gender are also common.

If any group members are openly gay, lesbian, or bisexual, you may want to invite them to talk about what that has meant for them in your setting, and what that has meant in regard to relationships. Be sure to ask them ahead of time if this is okay with them. Just because they are "out" doesn't mean that they want to be singled out to talk about it. Encourage the group to think of same-gender relationships in terms of affection, support, conversation, shared interests, and respect—not just in terms of sexual activity. Most of the questions in this session relate to any type of close, caring relationship, not just to heterosexual relationships.

133

objectives

- Students learn how their peers think and feel about going out socially.
- They learn about the attitudes of others in regard to romantic relationships.
- They explore their own dating relationships in the supportive environment of the group.

suggestions

1. Begin by asking:

   ▶ What advice or warnings have you received from your parents about going out with someone?

   ▶ (With a smile:) How much do you think about this subject?

2. Encourage discussion of the following topics and other similar topics:

   ▶ What are some family rules about going out?

   ▶ Think about your social group. What are their rules about going out with someone?

   ▶ How many of your friends are going out with someone now? How much do your friends do things together as a group? Is group activity mixed-gender?

   ▶ When two people are going out, who usually pays for movies, food, concert tickets, and so on?

   ▶ If one person pays for everyone on a date, what (if anything) is expected of the other person?

   ▶ Should males open doors for females?

   ▶ Do all females appreciate gifts and flowers? Do males?

   ▶ Who should be expected to make decisions when two people are going out regularly?

   ▶ How much are either males or females seen as "trophies"?

   ▶ Who makes the first move by asking the other person out? What are some ways to ask a person out?

   ▶ If the person who is asked doesn't want to accept, how should she (or he) say that?

   ▶ When should a relationship be ended?

3. Explain that the next few questions are for group members who are going out with someone regularly or who have gone out with someone regularly in the past. Then ask these questions, perhaps alternating between present and past tense to include discussion of past relationships:

   ▶ How have your parents reacted to the person you are going out with?

   ▶ How does their attitude—whether positive or negative—affect the relationship?

▶ What are some relationship issues the two of you should talk about?

▶ How well do you talk together about how each of you feels about the other's behavior?

▶ How able are you to assert yourself about your wishes?

▶ Can one member of a couple give in too much to the other—for example, in decisions about where to go, what to do, when to leave, when and how to show affection, etc.?

▶ If so, how can that affect the relationship over the short term and the long term?

4. For closure, ask for comments about how it felt to discuss romantic relationships in the group. Was it interesting? Helpful? Thought-provoking? Comfortable? Uncomfortable? Let their nods suffice. Thank the group for teaching you about their social world.

focus: relationships
gender behavior and sexual harassment

background

There is much confusion about what is expected of both males and females, not only in dating relationships, but also in other areas of life. New awareness about sexual harassment has highlighted confusion about appropriate vs. inappropriate behaviors in school, in the workplace, and in other environments and situations. Many marriages struggle with gender roles and expectations as well. The media continue to "teach" how to be male and female, significant adults may model gender behaviors that don't fit well in the current world, and the movement toward liberation of both genders causes many to feel unsure about what is proper and expected. Adolescents must sort out many messages about gender, sexuality, and relationships in general.

Our sense of who we are as sexual beings reflects cultural attitudes, expectations, and taboos about gender behavior. Our sexuality involves affection, attraction, intimacy, social behavior, and communication styles, among many aspects. It is appropriate to consider sexual and gender behavior in regard to relationships, and this session does that.

important

If this session takes place in a school or organizational setting, it's important for you to familiarize yourself in advance with the school's or organization's policies and procedures regarding sexual harassment. For example, if someone in your group describes a specific incident of sexual harassment, you will want to know about mandatory reporting and how to follow up. Your district or organization likely has guidelines specific to these issues. It is best to know them ahead of time.

recommended resource

Strauss, S., and P. Espeland. *Sexual Harassment and Teens: A Program for Positive Change* (Minneapolis: Free Spirit Publishing, 1992).
A comprehensive course in sexual harassment awareness and prevention, with background information that would be useful in a discussion.

objectives

- Students learn about gender differences in communication styles.
- They consider the importance of mutual respect between the genders.
- They consider some possible meanings, reasons, and effects of sexual harassment.

suggestions

1. Introduce the topic with material from "Background" and supplement it with information from books, newspapers, or magazines related to gender roles, sexual harassment, relationships, and communication styles, for example. Acknowledge that what we hear about gender behavior is often confusing.

2. Pursue the idea of communication differences between males and females. Ask the students if they believe the following statements are true. Invite comments on them. Several individuals in the behavioral sciences have made statements like these; however, remind the students that they do not have to agree. Encourage them to *consider* the thoughts presented. Obviously, no statement is true for *all* persons of one gender.

   - Women are good listeners. They respond supportively to what is said in conversation.
   - Men offer information and opinions, interrupt each other, and change topics in conversation.
   - Women finish each other's sentences in conversation. They perceive this as being supportive rather than rude. They stick with topics.
   - Men are concerned about independence, asserting themselves, and who is and isn't dominant. Conversation is about establishing turf. Men aren't used to having people agree with them.
   - Women are concerned about maintaining the relationship. Conversation is socially binding.
   - Men's voices are louder and more listened to in a group. They set the tempo of the group, and women adapt to the pace.
   - Women often feel as if they are not heard in mixed groups, including in corporate and professional meetings. They are not used to being given opportunities to talk. They give nonverbal signals of support. They smile more than men do in groups. They are influenced by others' opinions.
   - Even though students may prefer same-sex groups in the classroom, especially when they are young, they need to learn how to communicate effectively with the other gender by learning some of their techniques.

   Emphasize that these differences in how males and females communicate—whether great or small, consistently present or not—

can interfere with communication and comfort at home, at school, at work, and in couple relationships.

3. Explore the idea of sexual harassment by asking these questions:

   ▶ What does "sexual harassment" mean? (The key is that it is unwelcome and inappropriate, whether it takes the form of sexual advances, requests for sexual favors, or other behaviors that are sexual in nature. Sexual behavior that is welcome and appropriate is not harassment. Harassment does not have to be physical, dramatic, or threatening. Whether or not it is frequent, and even if it is only semi-uncomfortable, it may lead to uncomfortableness in that environment generally. The harasser is often someone in a more powerful position.)

   ▶ What kinds of communication from, and behaviors in, the other gender make you uncomfortable?

   ▶ What are some possible motives or reasons for comments and behaviors like those? (Power and control? Displaced/misplaced anger? Role-modeling that sent demeaning messages about the other gender, or about behavior in relationships?)

   ▶ Where do we learn how to behave toward men? Toward women? (Parents are probably every person's first role models in this regard—i.e., about how men and women treat each other. Other significant relatives, peers, and the media instruct as well. Stress that we can *un*learn those lessons by becoming sensitive to the effects of our behaviors and by practicing new behaviors.)

   ▶ Have you ever felt sexually harassed? (Be aware that males can also feel harassed. Respect such feelings and comments related to this question.)

   ▶ What was involved?

   ▶ What were your feelings?

   Emphasize that feelings can be strong, even if the harassment is subtle. People who are harassed often blame themselves; fear taunting or further harassment if they complain; wonder what the behavior means; feel powerless, embarrassed, ashamed, or trapped; and feel less free to be themselves. Point out that behaviors are practiced when young. Now is the time to be aware of them and to change them. The key to social ease and successful relationships is respect, not power and control over someone else.

4. For closure, ask the group to comment on whether the discussion was comfortable, appropriate, and/or beneficial. How did they feel during the discussion? What new thoughts and/or insights did they have? You might also summarize the concerns about sexual harassment you have heard in the group.

focus: relationships
sexual behavior

background

Adolescents think about relationships and sexual behavior a lot—some say most of the time! Adults probably underestimate this preoccupation. An entire year of discussion groups probably could be devoted to those two topics alone. And yet, the preoccupation doesn't mean that adolescents are well-informed about sexual behavior—even those who are sexually active. To provide at least a beginning of dialogue, this session offers students a chance to explore the topic of sexual behavior in a safe, supportive group setting.

important

You may want to invite a psychologist or therapist who relates well to adolescents to attend this session, perhaps responding to questions written anonymously, for the speaker, by group members at the end of the previous session. If you do not invite a speaker, use the students' written questions as discussion-starters yourself. (Or have students write their questions during this session, and then use them during a follow-up session.) Encourage them to pose questions they have often wondered about and would like to discuss in a safe, supportive environment, where there are no dumb questions.

Whatever the specific aspect of sexual behavior being addressed, it is a good idea to check out what students know *before* adding information or making comments. As always, assess maturity level carefully when deciding which resources or suggestions to use.

objectives

- Students have a safe place to ask questions about, and discuss, sexual behavior.
- They discover that they are not the only adolescents with questions about sexual behavior.
- They consider alternatives to being sexually active.

suggestions

1. Introduce the session with reference to "Background." Then ask this general question: "Do you remember something you once heard about sex and relationships that you now know wasn't correct?"

2. Hand out copies of "Sexual Behavior" (page 142) and ask the students to fill out the questionnaire with brief responses, anonymously. They can be as honest as they want to be. Use the questionnaire to generate discussion. If the group seems shy or inhibited, take a poll on several of the questions, and ask them to discuss the results.

3. Question #9 on the handout addresses sexual activity and offers an opportunity for extended discussion. Offer these as possible non-physical motivators, if they aren't mentioned:

   ▶ to discover more about the self

   ▶ to feel "adult"

   ▶ to combat loneliness or a sense of not belonging

   ▶ to express anger, to rebel, to escape problems

   ▶ as an expression of low self-esteem, self-punishment, self-loathing

   ▶ media messages

   ▶ peer pressure.

4. Question #10 might generate discussion. Might it be true that those who are *not* sexually active believe most others are? Might those who *are* active want to believe that most others are also? Ask these questions:

   ▶ How much bragging about sexual activity is there in your peer group?

   ▶ How much sexual activity do you think is really going on in your peer group?

   ▶ Without naming any names, how do you feel about your peers who are sexually active?

   ▶ How much is "safe sex" discussed in your peer group and in dating relationships?

   ▶ How much unsafe sex do you think there is in your peer group?

   ▶ In your opinion, is there a trend toward abstinence today in young adults? If so, what might be contributing to that trend? If not, why not?

   ▶ Is everyone confused and intrigued and somewhat apprehensive about sexual activity? Do young partners need to discuss those feelings with each other? (You might suggest that such communication is good preparation for communication in marriage and other relationships. It might also contribute to delaying sexual activity and to considering other options for activity.)

   ▶ If a couple can't talk about sex, should they be having it?

5. Question #11 deserves emphasis. Ask for the group members' answers, summarize their collective responses, and, perhaps ask these additional questions:

    ▶ Is alcohol used as an excuse for sexual behavior?

    ▶ Is alcohol used to take away inhibitions?

    ▶ To what extent is someone responsible for his or her sexual behavior, whether or not alcohol is involved?

6. Ask the group, "When you think of a creative dating experience, as one couple or with several couples in a group, with activities that are both fun and helpful for getting better acquainted, what comes to mind?" (Encourage the group to think beyond alcohol/drugs and sex.)

7. Bring up the topic of mixed messages. Ask the following:

    ▶ Do females sometimes send males mixed messages about their sexual interests—so that males are confused about what behavior is right, wanted, or appropriate?

    ▶ Give an example of such a message from a female.

    ▶ Do males sometimes send mixed messages—so that females feel confused?

    ▶ Give an example of such a message from a male.

8. For closure, summarize what you have heard in the discussion. You might emphasize that there is choice about sexual behavior. They are in charge of their choices. Even if they have chosen in the past to be sexually active, they can choose now to stop. Then ask the group how they felt during the discussion—comfortable/uncomfortable, amazed at the openness, relieved, fascinated, embarrassed? Collect and dispose of the questionnaires.

sexual behavior

1. Do you feel well-informed about sex? Yes ☐ No ☐
   Where have you gotten most of your information? _____
   If you had a personally important question about sex, who would you ask? _____
   If you had a choice between getting information from a respected, trusted adult or from your best friend, who would it be? _____

2. What are some ways to express affection with a partner—besides having sex?
   _____
   _____

3. What would you do if your date were insisting on sexual intercourse, and you did not feel ready for it in that relationship (or in general)? _____
   _____

4. Do you worry a lot about sexual matters? Yes ☐ No ☐

5. Do you worry about AIDS? Yes ☐ No ☐
   Do you worry about other sexually transmitted diseases? Yes ☐ No ☐

6. What do you think about *not* having sexual intercourse before marriage?
   _____
   Is that value important—and discussed—among your friends? Yes ☐ No ☐
   Is it a message worth listening to, in your opinion? Yes ☐ No ☐

7. What is the potential harm in having sexual intercourse at an early age?
   _____
   Before one is ready for it? _____
   _____
   Outside of a committed and mature relationship? _____
   _____

8. When is a person ready for sexual intercourse? _____
   _____

9. What are some of the reasons someone your age might be sexually active—besides sexual drive?
   _____
   _____

10. What percentage of males in your class do you believe are sexually active? _____
    What percentage of females? _____

11. Why should people be concerned about alcohol consumption in regard to social and sexual behavior? _____
    _____

focus: relationships
date rape

background

Only in recent years has date rape received more than passing attention as a serious social problem. Media attention to date and acquaintance rape (as opposed to rape by stereotypical strangers in dark alleys) is increasing, and campus health centers now display brochures about date rape. But it is still rarely reported. No one knows how prevalent it is, but campus surveys indicate that it is widespread. Even though most victims blame themselves for being naive, being too trusting, drinking, or not being able to control the situation, a lapse of discretion or safety precautions can never justify a rape. However, young women often are not enough aware of how those and other factors contribute to vulnerability. Even those who are not naive may find themselves unprepared and feeling defenseless in situations with sexually aggressive males.

Perhaps all women are vulnerable to date and acquaintance rape. It is even possible that achieving, intelligent, compliant females are especially vulnerable. The "good girl" self-concept may prevent a young woman from leaving, asserting herself, or even struggling or screaming at the time—and from seeking help after the fact. She might even be concerned about embarrassing the acquaintance. Most sexual attacks during junior or senior high school or on college campuses are made by someone the victim knows. Social upbringing often does not prepare a girl for sexual aggressiveness, and it often does not provide survival skills. New college students and young women in the working world, eager to make friends, need to be alert and wise in the social scene. No matter what the social situation, and no matter what their background, women of all ages and circumstances need to be aware of the problem of date and acquaintance rape. Assess the maturity level of your group carefully when considering this session, although beware of underestimating the vulnerability of even middle-school children.

important

If someone drops an emotional bombshell during the discussion about having been the victim of date/acquaintance rape or attempted rape, or if someone comes to you afterward and tells you about a date/acquaintance rape or attempted rape, be sure to have available a list of school and community resources to

143

contact for help/counseling. Whether or not you are a counselor, listen attentively and compassionately. It is probably difficult for the individual to talk about the experience, and it is appropriate to commend the person's courage in speaking of it. Remind the group about confidentiality.

objectives

- Both males and females will become more aware of the prevalence of date/acquaintance rape.

- Through discussing realistic situations, females will become wiser and less vulnerable to date/acquaintance rape, and males will become more informed and sensitive about it.

suggestions

1. Some group members will feel uncomfortable speaking about this subject, but most will be willing to discuss expectations, vulnerabilities, responsibilities, pressures, and socialization about masculinity and femininity. Introduce date/acquaintance rape as falling under the general category of "when-parents-worry-about-their-children-finding-themselves-in-situations-they-can't-handle." These general questions might be asked. Encourage group members to be discreet in answering.

   ▶ Does anyone have the right to demand intercourse under any circumstances?

   ▶ Without naming names, how prevalent is date rape in your age group, in your opinion?

   ▶ Have you ever been in a situation where sexual aggression caught you off guard?

   ▶ What do you know about the effects of date rape?

   ▶ What are some strategies for dealing with sexual aggression?

   ▶ What can contribute to date/acquaintance rape? (Alcohol, dress, being alone, intimidation, flirting, attitudes in both males and females?)

   ▶ What can someone do to be less vulnerable to it?

2. Brainstorm and discuss the differences among consensual (based on mutual consent), manipulated, coerced, and forced sex. Ask the group which ones are illegal (psychologically coerced or physically forced). Make the lists on a chalkboard, if one is available. Group members might suggest the following differences:

   ▶ Consensual sex probably involves smiles, closeness, affection, mutuality, comfort, and verbal and nonverbal communication.

   ▶ Manipulated sex might involve candlelight, perhaps alcohol, one person's planning and expectations, playing to the other's vulnerabilities, concern for the other person and the self, and all the aspects listed under "consensual."

- Coerced sex probably involves power and strength, guilt, threats, debt, and discomfort, and might involve alcohol and lies.

- Forced sex probably involves fear, fighting, physical touching unlike that related to consensual sex, aggression, threats, submission to survive (not consensual), and possibly momentary paralysis of movement.

3. Stress that women can minimize their vulnerability. Have the group make a list of recommendations. Suggestions might include:

- Think through the limits you want to set on sexual behavior prior to going out.

- Express feelings honestly and communicate assertively and with certainty.

- Pay attention to what you wear and make sure that your verbal and nonverbal messages agree—and that they agree with your intent.

- Don't leave a friend alone in a situation where she is vulnerable.

- Don't give in to pressure to have sexual intercourse or give it to return a favor.

4. Create some scenarios for the group to discuss and problem-solve, or hand out copies of "Problem Scenarios" (pages 146–147). You will probably want to emphasize what makes the person vulnerable in each situation. The last three scenarios involve males, two as a potential victim and one as the aggressor. Your group might want to discuss more situations where males feel uncomfortable about sexual activity or are in situations where they perceive intercourse is expected.

   For Scenario A, encourage the students to address the issue of the young woman's wish to talk at the point when she learns that the young man's parents are gone for the weekend. For Scenario B, pay attention to the vulnerability of the girlfriend. Scenario F was written with a female in mind, but if someone mentions that the rape victim could be male, explore that possibility.

5. For closure, tell the students what you have heard them say, in general, or have one or two of them summarize what has been discussed. Compliment them for handling the discussion well or for articulating difficult matters, if appropriate. Stress that if they are ever raped, they should seek help immediately, report the rape, be examined, and be counseled. This is also true in cases of attempted rape. Counseling will be important, since feelings about self-worth, sexuality, and relationships undoubtedly will be affected. Many who are raped do not report the attack because they blame themselves for losing control of the situation. Remind the group that loss of control *never* justifies one person forcing sex on another. In addition, warn them about making false accusations. More than just the accused can be harmed.

problem scenarios

A. You, a young woman, have been dating someone casually for a few weeks, but you do not feel committed to the relationship and have strong reservations about having sex with him. You enjoy talking with him. In fact, he is the first person you have dated who is interesting to talk with. You look forward to the conversations. After a movie and pizza, which he paid for, he asks if you would like to see where he lives with his parents. You arrive at his home, he asks if you would like some wine, you say yes, and then he tells you that his parents are gone for the weekend.

B. You and a girlfriend attend a community dance in a nearby town. You are wearing a low-cut blouse and a narrow skirt with a long slit on one side. A handsome guy, apparently in his early twenties, dances with you, and you enjoy flirting and dancing with him for most of the night. You would like to go out with him again. He asks if he can take you home. You see that your girlfriend is also quite occupied with someone. You leave with him.

C. You are a young woman at a party with many of your friends. There is alcohol, and everyone is drinking. Some are dancing, some are disappearing, and you are beginning to feel a bit drunk. You are dancing with someone you've been casually involved with for a week or two.

D. You are an attractive college freshman woman and are attending a dance sponsored by your sorority and a fraternity. It is your first college dance. You are not naive about sexual behavior (in fact, you and your former boyfriend were sexually active during your senior year in high school before you broke up), but you are uneasy about what you have heard are the sexual expectations of this particular fraternity. You are getting a lot of attention from a senior.

E. You have never considered yourself to be a physically attractive female. In fact, you are quite self-conscious. Your strengths are, you feel, your intellect and your ability to read others well, to be nice to everyone, and not to be confrontational and demanding. You were surprised when you were invited to join a sorority of the "beautiful ones." One night, your sorority has a party. A good-looking, fairly smooth guy asks you to dance. You are flattered when he dances with you for the next four dances, even though you wonder if maybe someone has dared him to, and he seems overly complimentary. He radiates confidence and sexuality. The dance is nearly over, and he's asking to take you to his friend's apartment, where some of his friends "probably are."

F. You were raped by an acquaintance three nights ago after a party. You are uneasy about telling even your best friend, since you feel that you shouldn't have let yourself be vulnerable, and you know that the acquaintance has a great amount of credibility. You are very upset, feel violated and depressed, are shaky, and haven't slept much since then.

G. You are a female commuter college student and need to make a phone call, but you have no change. You know several people in a coed dormitory and decide to stop to call there. In the lobby, you see a male you've met in a class, and you tell him about your need to call. He invites you to use the phone in his room.

H. You have not dated much, even though you are a high-school senior—a conscientious, fairly quiet guy who doesn't feel comfortable at parties and is shy around girls. An aggressive, sexually experienced girl asks you to dance at the first party you have attended all year. She seems to have taken on the responsibility of instructing you in sexual behavior. You and she are now in the back of her friend's pick-up truck. You feel quite uncomfortable about the way things are going, but you are aroused and feel unable to leave the situation. You are very concerned about what she might think of you—no matter what you might say right now.

I. You are a sexually experienced young male. A beautiful woman your age has accepted an invitation to come to your apartment for a drink after a party. You know that she is not inexperienced sexually, because you know others who have dated her. She is also enticingly dressed and has been flirting with you quite obviously. The two of you have been kissing on the sofa, but she has said she wants to go home now, and when you persist with more physical aggression, she begins to cry.

J. You are a respected college sophomore male, known for your athletic achievements. You have been in a relationship with a female classmate. You are quite sure you have never behaved improperly with her. She was very upset when you quietly told her last night that you wanted to break up. Today you heard she is claiming that you raped her. She might even press charges.

focus: relationships
patterns of violence and abuse

background

According to the media, violence among teen couples appears to be rising. Therefore, the topic of violence certainly deserves more attention than just one session. It can be connected to the sessions in Focus: Feelings on "Mood Range," "Anger," and "Sadness and Depression." It can be looked at with statistical information, in the context of our changing society, as a response to violence in the media, as connected to role modeling, or as a power and control issue, among many possible approaches. This session will focus on just one aspect of violence—abusive relationships.

The purpose of this session is to help students understand that abusive relationships occur at all levels of society, in all age groups, and are perpetuated from one generation to the next. Both genders learn how to treat a partner, and what to expect from a partner, by observing the adults in their lives. Often, people stay in abusive situations because they learned young to accept abuse. Unfortunately, many in such relationships do not feel they can do anything to help themselves. They fear what the abuser might do if they leave, or they doubt their ability to manage alone. They believe they have no choice but to stay in the relationship.

Changes in the response to abuse and in beliefs about the self might, in fact, provoke changes in the abuser, depending on the kind of abuse and the depth of the pattern. Abusers have the same task—to take steps to change patterns of response to stressful situations and beliefs about themselves and others. Raised awareness through discussion may encourage a young abuser to seek help or to take personal stock and stop an early habit, or encourage abused individuals to seek help. Unless changes are made, the abuse will continue. Options beyond individual change for someone being abused include individual or couple counseling to take stock of the relationship in general and examine abusive sequences, crisis centers, leaving the relationship, or all of these. Of prime importance for adolescents is awareness that marriage does not cure an abusive dating relationship.

important

This session encourages an honest look at abusive relationships that may help to prevent them or give students courage to leave them. Although you should be prepared for the possibility that students may share experiences with past or current abuse, that is not the intent here. Some students in abusive situations may seek you out individually as well. Be aware of laws regarding mandatory reporting before addressing this issue in the group, inform the group about limits of confidentiality in that regard, and be clear about the purpose of your group. If sensitive information is shared, discreetly or indiscreetly, remind the group about the rules of confidentiality. There can be value in this particular session without self-revelation.

You might plan to feature a speaker from a domestic violence shelter or center, or from a mental health agency. If so, you will need to make these arrangements in advance of this session. Also, you probably will want to find out what your community offers by way of counseling resources, in case you choose to make a general recommendation or are asked privately for information about such resources.

objectives

- Students learn that abuse can occur in relationships at all levels of society and in all age groups.

- They learn that patterns of abuse can become firmly established in a relationship, and that stopping them requires courage and conscious effort.

suggestions

1. If you have arranged for a speaker to visit your group, open the session by inviting him or her to present information about abusive relationships and helpful suggestions for avoiding or stopping them. The focus could be on patterns that become established early in relationships, even for adolescents, or on factors that contribute to violent and abusive behavior and to vulnerability to abuse.

2. In addition to, or in place of, hearing the speaker's presentation, group members can respond to the following statements. You might type the statements on separate pieces of paper and have group members read them in turn. Ask them whether the statements are believable.

   ▶ Abuse means dominance, power, control, and victimization.

   ▶ Abuse can happen at all levels of society—even among people of high wealth and status.

   ▶ Abuse can be physical, verbal, or emotional. The abused person can be either male or female. Females are more likely to abuse verbally than physically. Verbal and emotional abuse, by either gender, may actually be harder to stop than physical abuse.

   ▶ Victims of abuse may believe they are responsible for others' behavior and accept blame for causing the abuse.

   ▶ People who are abused may believe they don't deserve good things.

> ▶ People who are abused fear "rocking the boat."

> ▶ People who are abused often do not believe that they have options.

> ▶ Both abusers and their victims may fear and numb their emotions.

> ▶ People who are abused may fear their abusers so much that they are reluctant to force changes.

> ▶ People who are abused believe *they* are the ones who need to be better. Abusers sense that.

> ▶ Abusers and their victims both may fear rejection.

> ▶ People who are abused might keep picking abusers for partners because they have confused love with abuse.

> ▶ Men and women are often attracted to the *pattern* they grew up with. If their experiences contributed to positive self-esteem, and if they experienced and witnessed healthy relationships, they will probably be attracted healthily. We learn by observation how couples are "supposed to" behave.

> ▶ People who were abused in the past can become abused *or* abusive. Suffering abuse early in life can be seen as punishment or proof of low worth. That abuse can make someone vulnerable to abuse in relationships later in life.

> ▶ Victimization and abusive behaviors are "trained." Both can be changed with effort and assistance.

> ▶ The emptiness of abusive relationships leaves people vulnerable to addictions, because the emptiness wants to be filled by something. Alcohol and other drugs may be used to fill the emptiness.

3. Ask the group how they would know if they were in an abusive relationship. (Possible responses: being hit, shoved, or slapped; being constantly or frequently criticized; feeling controlled; being physically or psychologically coerced to have sex, or to behave in other ways that are contrary to personal values.)

   Brainstorm options for avoiding and stopping abuse. Emphasize that everyone in the group is worthy of respect and kindness in relationships. They do not "make" anyone treat them badly. Inform them that groups to help abusive partners are common, and that individual or group counseling can be effective in changing patterns. This information is important for all future relationships.

4. For closure, summarize and thank the speaker and commend the students for their attentiveness and comments. If there was no speaker, summarize the discussion. Emphasize again that they do not deserve abuse in *any* situation, including dating relationships, and that abusive behavior is *never* appropriate or justified.

focus: relationships
marriage

background

Some adolescents have doubts about marriage. Perhaps they have seen sadness in their parents' relationship, the impact of divorce or spousal abuse, or the tensions of employment brought home. They are probably aware of the challenges of raising children. They might even wonder if they will, can, or should marry. In contrast, some adolescents continue to have a romantic, love-conquers-all, living-happily-ever-after view of marriage. They expect to find a perfect partner, who will be everything to them forever, and have beautiful kids, house, car, and lifestyle. Obviously, there are attitudes all along a continuum.

This session offers adolescents a chance to sort out the real, the ideal, and the feared. Be aware that if a variety of cultures or religious backgrounds are represented in your group, there may be a variety of values and opinions expressed in the discussion. Such open exchange can contribute not only to affirmation of diversity, but also to an appreciation for the unique support for marriage and family built into many cultures.

objectives

- Students articulate their attitudes and thoughts about marriage.
- They consider the impact of the media on their expectations about marriage, and the impact of their own experiences on their attitudes and concerns about marriage.

suggestions

1. Invite the group to define "marriage." Expect that some might mention lesbian and gay relationships, and some might feel that commitment without official sanction constitutes a marriage. Ask one or more of these questions:

    ▶ What makes a marriage?

    ▶ Is there a difference between "marriage" and "just living together"? (Expect that this question might provoke strong disagreement. Consider the theme of Suggestion #4 below.)

    ▶ What might be gained by living *alone* before marriage? (Developing a sense of self, management skills, competence, and

151

independence—to make an unhealthy level of dependence less likely in marriage later.)

2. Steer the discussion toward the students' feelings about marriage.

   ▶ Are you idealistic about marriage?

   ▶ What do you expect in a marriage partner?

   ▶ What anxieties or fears do you have about marriage?

   ▶ Are you optimistic or pessimistic about being able to sustain a marriage relationship?

   ▶ Where might your optimism or pessimism come from?

3. Ask the group what makes it difficult to sustain marriages in the current world. They might mention some of these factors in society:

   ▶ dual-career couples, with more daily people-contact for both spouses than in the past and heavy time and energy demands

   ▶ economic self-sufficiency for some women, giving them options when their marriages are unhappy

   ▶ less stigma associated with divorce than previously

   ▶ unrealistic expectations of marriage

   ▶ lack of commitment to relationships

   ▶ no skills in conflict resolution (and no role modeling for it)

   ▶ geographic mobility, with no extended family or long-term friends available for support

   ▶ high stress and poor coping skills

   ▶ money problems

   ▶ partners growing and changing in different ways and at different speeds

   ▶ longer life spans, with marriages tested over a longer period

   ▶ overcommitment to work and community, with resulting physical and emotional exhaustion, making couple-contact minimal and/or strained

   ▶ males being socialized in ways that don't encourage expression of feelings

   ▶ females expecting their needs to be met without verbalizing them

   ▶ the distractions and commitment of raising children

   ▶ females with double job/home duties, with the spouse (who may not help with domestic chores) feeling neglected

   ▶ the fact that both partners bring psychological "baggage" into the marriage

   ▶ couples not seeking counseling from an objective professional when there are problems or not seeking it early enough.

4. Discuss commitment. Ask the group the following questions:

   ▶ What does "commitment" mean?

   ▶ Is commitment the difference between marriage and just living together?

   ▶ How much is commitment role modeled today? Is there a couple you know or can think of that seems like a good role model for commitment?

   ▶ What does commitment have to do with working through problems?

   ▶ Do all successful relationships involve give-and-take, ups and downs?

   ▶ Does our mainstream society "train" us to compete rather than cooperate? (Some non-mainstream cultures have a cooperative, collaborative, networking value-orientation and may be less vulnerable to divorce than the mainstream, with its competitive, individualistic value-orientation.)

   ▶ Are people "trained" to blame others when they have problems?

5. Focus on what kinds of images the various media present about marriage. Ask these questions:

   ▶ What are some TV-soap-opera images? Disney-movie images? Fairy-tale images? Movie-star images? TV-sitcom images? Romance-novel images? Popular-movie images? Magazine images?

   ▶ How do these images affect a young person's expectations of marriage?

   ▶ How do they affect the ability to sustain a marriage—or attitudes about commitment?

   ▶ Do you think people are unprepared for the everyday? For the inconvenient? For the realities of making a living?

6. Focus on expectations by asking these questions:

   ▶ What expectations are appropriate for the marriage relationship?

   ▶ Does everyone bring into marriage a fantasized belief that all needs will be taken care of?

   ▶ Does that expectation put too much pressure on the spouse—to "be everything"?

   ▶ Who else can "be something" for a person who is married?

   ▶ How many sources of support (people, family, activities, work) does a person need to stay "balanced"?

7. For closure, thank the group for sharing their feelings and insights. How did it feel to discuss marriage in their group? Ask someone to summarize the discussion or assess group consensus about marriage.

focus
the future

focus: the future

Students often hear that school is "preparation for life." They probably have heard all through school that they should do well—so they will have success at the next stage, which, they hear, is more important. So junior high or middle school becomes just preparation for high school, which is just preparation for trade school or college, which is just preparation for graduate school or another next step, which is...? Their parents might also perpetually speak in terms of "when we get this done, we can relax and really *live*."

Looking at each successive stage as preparation for something yet to come means that no stage is seen as real life, the life that is longed for. Each stage, in fact, is life—to be lived. *In the present.* The "dessert" may not be there in the end. The savory tastes of the main course may be missed, too, if attention is only on what is yet to come.

Then there are those who spend too little time being concerned about the future. They live only in the present. They may be impulsive and spontaneous in the extreme, unpracticed in delayed gratification, procrastinating with important preparation for the future, closing doors with unwise choices, resisting advice, and perhaps seeing little value in school and other responsibilities.

How can adolescents find middle ground? How can they focus on the future without becoming anxiety-ridden and joyless? How can they relax and enjoy the present without letting it blot out concern for what is coming? This final section offers sessions to help students focus appropriately on the future. It is good to talk about it with a comfortable group of peers.

general objectives

- Students look realistically into the future, while understanding the importance of living in the present.
- They look at themselves as moving along a continuum of development.
- They contemplate direction, meaning, and change.

156

focus: the future
open to change

background

Everyone responds to change uniquely. Some people embrace it eagerly and even seek it out and provoke it in their lives. When life becomes static, they feel they are in a rut and may make dramatic changes. Others resist change, or strenuously avoid it. They like life to be predictable and familiar. Most people fall somewhere along the continuum between these extremes. This session provides an opportunity to examine attitudes about change and the ability to cope with it.

objectives

- Students evaluate their ability to embrace change by looking at past changes in their lives.

- They think about significant changes that might occur in the next few years and consider their possible reactions to them.

suggestions

1. Introduce the discussion by referring to the ideas in "Background." Go around the group and invite members to finish this statement about their usual responses to change: "When there is a major change in my life, I usually react by _____." Then ask these two questions:

    ▶ Do you thrive on change or have anxiety about it?

    ▶ How confident are you that everything will eventually work out when you are faced with changes in your life?

2. Ask the students to give examples of changes in their lives. (If they seem to have difficulty with the idea of change, steer them in the direction of life adjustments, positive or negative: illness or accident, birth of a sibling, a death in the family, divorce, remarriage of a parent, moving to a new location, beginning junior high, beginning high school, a change in friends, an occurrence where trust in someone was lost, a family event.) Follow that with some of these questions:

    ▶ How did you respond to the change?

    ▶ (For those who had difficulty) How long did the adjustment period last?

157

▶ (If they eventually adjusted) When did you know you had coped with the change successfully?

▶ What had you done to help the process?

▶ Who are your role models for adjusting to change? How do these people adjust to change, generally?

▶ (For those who have dealt well with change:) What strategies do you use for coping with change?

3. If you think your group would enjoy it and gain from it, ask those who have trouble adjusting to change to give a detailed "recipe" for how to have difficulty with changes. That request may sound bizarre, but it will give those members an opportunity to speak as if they have control over their responses to change. Allow them to create their own examples; illustrate with one or more of the following only if necessary:

▶ Be angry. Find someone to blame for the change.

▶ Resist the change with all of your energy.

▶ Become depressed.

▶ Do something to show how bad the change is—sulk, run away, make life miserable for others.

▶ Believe wholeheartedly that you will never adjust to the change.

▶ Believe that nothing good will come of the change.

▶ Lie awake at night and think of ways to change things back to how they were.

▶ Get physically ill.

▶ Change your personality so that no one will see how you used to be.

4. Encourage group members to anticipate changes in the future by asking these questions:

▶ What changes do you anticipate in your family in the next year? Two years? Five years?

▶ What changes do you anticipate in yourself in the next year? Two years? Five years?

▶ Can you anticipate all of the changes that might happen in your life?

▶ What kinds of changes do you think you will have the most trouble coping with and adjusting to?

▶ What can you do for yourself during the time of change?

▶ What can you rely on if there is a major, surprising change? (Your experience in life. Knowing you have survived changes in the past. Your ability to adjust.)

5. For closure, ask someone to summarize the discussion or give a one-sentence suggestion for how to change successfully, based on the discussion. What feelings did group members have during the discussion as memories were evoked, or as members shared their thoughts? Did it feel safe to have those feelings in the group?

focus: the future
what is maturity?

objectives

- Students learn that maturity is a nebulous concept that means different things to different people.

- They apply the term to both adolescent and adult behavior.

- They appreciate the ways they feel mature and realize that they are *in the process* of gaining maturity.

- They have fun discussing a term that is often used to point out what they are *not*.

suggestions

1. Ask the students to define "maturity," orally or in writing. Then ask them to explain what they think various age groups mean when they use the term: teens, parents, employers, teachers, the elderly.

2. Then pursue these strands:
   - When do you feel mature now?
   - When do you not feel mature now?
   - When will you know you are finally mature?

3. Ask the students if others often comment about their being or not being mature.
   - (For those who often hear that they are mature:) What effect has that had on you?
   - (For those who often hear that they are immature:) What effect has that had on you?

4. Invite them to consider the following:
   - What is "immature" behavior?
   - Can adults be immature? If so, give some examples of immature adult behavior.
   - What is the upside of being mature? Of being immature?
   - What is the downside of being mature? Of being immature?

5. Move the discussion to the topic of late maturers.
   - What is meant by the term "late maturing"?

> ▸ Do you think you are ahead, behind, or right on schedule in maturing?

Offer this statement: "Early physical maturity often has a negative affect on girls socially, and a positive effect on boys." (Berk, 1991.) Follow that with these questions:

> ▸ Do you think that statement is true?

> ▸ Has it been true for you?

> ▸ How much do you think late physical maturity affects girls and boys academically?

> ▸ Do you think early or late physical maturity affects success in life? How?

6. For closure, thank and compliment the group for their insights and comments, and either summarize the session yourself or ask a student to do that.

reference   Berk, L. E. *Child Development* (Boston: Allyn & Bacon, 1991).

focus: the future
finding meaning

This session is appropriate for adolescents who are capable of dealing with the abstractness of "meaning." Be aware that even very young adolescents, when they have high ability, sometimes struggle seriously with meaning. They wonder what life is about, what their purpose is on the planet, why they were born. They want to understand those things—now. Sometimes they despair because they do not understand. They may even wonder if life is worth living. Their parents, if they are aware of these thoughts, sometimes become frightened about their children's heavy and precocious thoughts.

Older adolescents may struggle with the same questions, but some, by then, have found meaning and purpose through involvement in satisfying activities, in relationships, or in contribution to society. Sometimes they have found it through adversity.

Is that, in fact, how meaning is found—through involvement, experiences, relationships, struggle? Do struggle and experiences contribute to "material," which is woven into interestingly textured fabric, which makes a personal tapestry, which is identity, which is story, which has meaning? That is only one attempt to make sense of meaning. How do individuals in your group see it?

objectives

- Students gain skills in articulating thoughts about purpose and meaning.

- They ponder "meaning"—whether it exists, and if so, if it comes through thought, action, struggle, or simply existing.

suggestions

1. Introduce the topic by asking the following questions, being careful to offer no definitions. Use the first two closed questions to provide thinking time and to set the stage for discussion. Nods may indicate a common concern. Don't rush these questions.

   ◗ Have you ever struggled with "meaning"—as in "the meaning of life" or "the meaning of existence"?

   ◗ Has that ever distressed you?

162

> Do you think meaning is worth worrying about? Why or why not?

> Have you ever come to any conclusions about purpose and meaning? If so, what are some of your conclusions?

> How have you changed your mind about these issues as you have matured?

2. Explore meaning in life by asking these questions:

> What makes life feel good and satisfying?

> What might help a retired person feel that life has had—and still has—meaning?

> What adults do you know who seem to feel a sense of meaning and/or purpose?

> What adults do you know who seem to feel great satisfaction in their work?

> What seems to be the most important thing in life, judging by adults you know:

  - a satisfying job?
  - a satisfying relationship?
  - children?
  - money?
  - health?
  - status?

Have group members rank the above six items from most to least important in regard what they believe contributes to life satisfaction, generally.

3. If your group members are older adolescents and/or have high ability, ask this question:

> If, in fact, a person does find meaning in life, how does this happen?

If group members do not mention ideas like those suggested in the third paragraph of "Background," you might bring them up at this point. Then continue with these questions:

> What do you think about the idea of pain and struggle leading to meaning?

> Do struggles in life have value? What important lessons might they teach? How might they teach us about ourselves?

> How might we find out who we are through being tested and finding our limits?

> How might struggles connect a person to the rest of humanity?

The following two closed questions are meant to be rhetorical and to provoke thought. Give the group time to ponder them. There is no "right" answer here or to any of the questions in this section.

▶ Do you think we might find meaning through connection to people?

▶ Do you think meaning might come through discoveries about ourselves?

Continue by asking these questions:

▶ Do you think meaning comes from being—or from doing?

▶ How much do you think meaning is related to doing what we feel we should be doing?

▶ Do we feel it when we are simply in the process of living, or do we have to have accomplished something specific to feel it?

▶ How much do you think knowing purpose and meaning is related to having a satisfying life?

▶ Do you think meaning has anything to do with being happy?

▶ Do you think a mid-life crisis might be partly about purpose and meaning? If so, in what way?

4. For closure, ask how it felt to discuss this abstract notion with the group. Was it discouraging, inspiring, frustrating, or energizing? What did they feel as various group members offered their thoughts? Was the discussion thought-provoking? Let nods suffice as responses to this last question.

focus: the future
anxiety

It is normal to feel anxiety when facing new or challenging situations. Someone might fear that a performance will not measure up, or sense that an impending decision might change life negatively, or worry about inadequacy in a relationship, or worry about the vague unknown ahead. When anxiety is a catalyst for growth, it is productive. The quality of life can be improved, and progress can be made. On the other hand, when anxiety preoccupies someone to the point of debilitation, it is unproductive. When a person is able to deal with anxiety, and not run from situations through escapism, addictions, or hysteria, and not shrink from the prospect of new challenges, life can be exciting and full of adventure. When anxiety is feared and avoided because it is unsettling, much of life's freedom is lost. Life satisfaction is probably related to the ability to adapt to change. Being able to deal with anxiety is part of being adaptable.

Adolescents of all ages experience anxiety. For some, it might be a constant, vague dread of what might lie ahead. For others, it might be worry about specific upcoming events. Perfectionists often are anxious about the next challenge, which, of course, must be done excellently. Many students with high ability worry about college selection and acceptance, which relates to academic and extracurricular performance, which relates to the papers and tests next week, which relate to the work schedule, relationship problems, and fatigue this week. They and others who may be chronically concerned about the unknown ahead may have difficulty relaxing in the present. Every action may seem momentous and heavily weighted. Feeling fragmented by too many commitments, and being preoccupied with personal problems, may make it hard to imagine getting over all the hurdles between present and future. And, of course, those are seen as a formidable whole, not as a series of conquerable, manageable steps.

For all students, there may also be anxiety about relationships ending, getting along at work, parents divorcing, parental unemployment, or financial problems. Even though worry is not grinding their lives to a halt, they need encouragement to pause and appreciate the present—and even laugh a little about themselves and their anxieties. Helping them to gain

165

insight about personal responses to various situations can also be beneficial. In this anxious era, they need to name their dread. They need to accept normal anxiety as potentially motivating and find ways to lessen whatever anxiety depletes energy and limits life.

objectives

- Students learn that having anxiety is part of being human.
- They practice articulating feelings and concerns about the future.
- They distinguish between productive and unproductive anxiety.

suggestions

1. To begin, ask someone to define "anxiety." Then invite the group to share what they worry about by asking, "What are vague worries that occupy your thoughts at various times, day or night?" Perhaps each group member can share three things.

2. Going around the group, ask each student to rate his or her general anxiety/worry level on a scale of 1–10 and report it to the group. Afterward, ask them to explain whether their anxiety is mostly about specific situations or is mostly vague. Ask them how much their anxiety affects their lives:

   - How much does your anxiety keep you from doing things that would actually help to relieve your anxiety?

   - How much of your free time is spent thinking anxious thoughts?

   - What are the catastrophes you worry about—terrible things that might happen if you do or don't do certain things? (Ask, "And *then* what would happen?... And *then* what would happen?" etc., to help them see how they have "catastrophized.")

   - Is what you are anxious about crucial to your life? How much does your personal well-being depend on these things?

   - (Encourage them to loosen up narrow thinking about future possibilities:) Do you have to know *now* how everything will turn out someday?

   - (Ask those with low levels of anxiety:) How do you/would you view some of the worry-filled situations the others have shared? What advice would you give them?

3. Introduce the idea of "productive anxiety"—worry that helps people get a job done, do what they need to do, and take care of personal care and safety. Ask the following:

   - What are some things you worry about that help you get things done that you need to do? (Assignments? Tests? Locking the door at night? Not losing your wallet or house key? Preparing for a performance?)

   - Can you think of some examples of excessive, unproductive worry? (Social situations in general? "What ifs"—like moving, parents divorcing, fire, natural disasters, death, not measuring up in the future, finding someone to marry, getting sick? Criticism? Imperfection? Mistakes?)

4. Ask them to think of several things they felt very anxious about a year ago. They might even write them down so that they can study them for a moment. Then ask these questions:

   ▶ How many of those situations turned out all right?

   ▶ Which ones were not worth worrying about? (They can have confidence that similar situations in the future will also work out all right.)

5. Invite the group to think about whether worry and anxiety can be learned. Ask:

   ▶ Who are your role models for worry and anxiety? Where might you have learned to worry as you do (whatever the level, whether productively or unproductively)?

6. Turn the group's attention to self-talk as a tool for coping with anxiety. Begin by asking these questions:

   ▶ What are some things you tell yourself when you are facing situations that are frightening? What goes through your head?

   ▶ What are some things you could tell yourself that might help you to handle these situations better?

   Expand on the idea of changing anxious self-talk to positive self-talk in certain situations. Encourage the group to come up with positive, rational statements to replace the following:

   ▶ "I've got to get an A on this test."

   ▶ "I'm not going to be able to remember what to say."

   ▶ "I'll be crushed if she says 'no.'"

   ▶ "I know I'm not going to do well in the game."

   ▶ "If I don't get that job, I'll have a miserable summer."

   ▶ "If we have to move, I'll never see my friends again."

   ▶ "If we move, I'll never make new friends."

   ▶ "If I don't have a date for prom, I'll never be able to show my face in school again."

   ▶ "If we break up, I'm going to die."

7. For closure, ask someone to summarize the session. Wish them a relaxing, only-productively-anxious time until the next meeting.

focus: the future
gender roles

- Students anticipate possible gender roles in their future.
- They consider how gender expectations affect job and career, family responsibilities, and lifestyle.

1. Ask the group, "What kind of woman/man will you be?" If they don't address the following areas spontaneously, follow up with these questions:

   ▶ What kind of life will you lead?

   ▶ Do you think you will be a "traditional" male? A "traditional" female? What do you think "traditional" will mean when you are an adult?

   ▶ Do you think you will marry early in life? Later in life? Or not at all?

   ▶ Do you think you will have children?

   ▶ Will you stop your career when children are born or ask for maternity/paternity leave?

   ▶ What kind of parenting arrangement will you be comfortable with?

   ▶ What kinds of interests will you have?

   ▶ What will you do to relax?

   ▶ Will you have skills and interests similar to those of your same-gender parent?

   ▶ Will you share household duties, like cooking, laundry, grocery-buying, paying bills, yard work, mechanical fixing, etc., with your partner?

   ▶ Will you be a "homebody," preferring to relax at home rather than going out?

   ▶ Will you stay fit?

▶ Will you be dependent on your spouse/partner and others for intellectual stimulation and emotional uplifting, or will you be relatively independent and self-sufficient?

▶ Will you be a "macho man"/"feminine woman" or a male/female with a different kind of attitude and personal style? Will you resist or welcome changes in gender roles?

You might also want to address the above questions one at a time and in depth.

2. Ask the group members some or all of these questions:

▶ What are your career plans?

▶ What training or education will be required?

▶ If you plan to have children, when would you like to have them?

▶ Do you anticipate any problems with job entrance or advancement in your chosen field because of your gender?

Ask the female group members how they feel about the aspirations of the male group members. Do they seem realistic, idealistic, or naive?

Ask the male group members how they feel about the aspirations of the female group members. Do they seem realistic, idealistic, or naive?

3. Encourage the group to explore their gender role expectations (and stereotypes) by asking the following:

▶ Would you feel comfortable being supervised, managed, or directed at work by a member of the other gender? By a member of the same gender?

▶ Would you resent a coworker's maternity/paternity leave if it required major adjustments in your own workload?

4. Invite the group to brainstorm some of the problems faced by dual-career couples. Mention the following if they don't come up during the brainstorming:

job transfers	commuting
child-rearing	division of labor at home
conflicting schedules	mutual exhaustion
little time together	different income levels

Then ask questions like these:

▶ How would you deal with your spouse's job transfer, if it meant you had to leave a good position?

▶ If you had children, what would be your role in child-rearing?

▶ When your schedules conflicted, whose schedule would be most important?

▶ If both of you worked outside the home, would you do half of the housework? More? Less? How would you determine what an appropriate level for you would be?

5. Invite the group to project into the future by asking the following:

   ▶ What do you think men's and women's roles will be when you are an adult—at home, in the workplace, in the community, and in state and national leadership?

   ▶ How will these roles be different from today?

   ▶ Have gender roles changed much in your lifetime? How?

   ▶ Will your role and attitudes be similar to those of your same-gender parent?

6. For closure, ask the group how they feel when they discuss gender roles. How do they feel when they think about changes in gender roles—excited? discouraged? apprehensive? scared?

focus: the future
making career choices

background

Most students with enough ability to consider continuing their education and having a career have considered more than one option. This session will focus on the "dilemma of choice." It is appropriate for all students, but is especially helpful to those who may have stress from "over-choice"— being able to do several things well, having many interests, and having the skills and motivation necessary to succeed in a number of areas. This may be true even for the underachiever who has many talents, but little motivation. Even a lack of motivation might be the result of being unable to find direction.

In addition, these adolescents are often burdened by the expectations of others. They hear a lot about their potential. They receive advice about careers, and the advice is often conflicting. Should they consider engineering, just because they are good in math and science? Should they avoid the arts, even though that is where their passion is, just because significant adults warn that they won't make a lot of money? Should they put job security first? How do they choose which interest they should take seriously? Should they consider combining interests? Could a major interest become a satisfying avocation or hobby?

When individuals have several abilities and options, other aspects than ability should be considered, such as personality, personal needs, dreams, and even values. (See Focus: Family, "Family Values," for more on this topic.) Sorting through these areas can be helpful in moving toward a clearer focus.

The job market will be different when these adolescents are ready to enter it. Some predict that there will be jobs for them, since they are a proportionately small group in the population as compared to the baby boomers. No one can predict exactly what the economy will be like, or what new job opportunities there will be, when today's adolescents are ready for their careers. But they are a generation that can probably take some risks and pursue their dreams.

This session is probably most appropriate for older adolescents, but the first four suggestions have been used successfully with above-average middle-school students. Even for the non-college-bound, this session can be valuable for personal assessment.

171

important

An option that can work well for a discussion group is to arrange in advance to have one or more persons from the community visit the group and speak about finding satisfying careers. Try to find middle-aged people of both genders who have made thoughtful and purposeful career *changes* in order to address the issue of "good fit." If your group includes students at risk, who may include high-ability underachievers, locate speakers who once were "square pegs in round holes," but who became successful as adults. Prepare a list of questions ahead of time for the students to use when interviewing the visitors; for ideas, see Suggestion #3.

objectives

- Students sort out personality factors, personal needs, lifestyle dreams, and a multitude of thoughts about careers.

- They learn that it is important to pay attention to personality and personal needs for the sake of life satisfaction as adults.

- They learn that there is probably no perfect career choice for them, and that there are probably several possibilities worthy of consideration.

- They learn that change is part of life and growth, and that education and adulthood might include changes in direction.

suggestions

1. Hand out copies of "Choosing a Career" (page 175) and ask the students to complete the questionnaire. Afterward, have them share their responses. (They might indicate by a show of hands who has chosen which responses for #2 and #3.) Ask questions like these:

   ▶ Do your responses for #2 and #3 match the careers you listed in #1?

   ▶ Does your lifestyle description for #6 match anything on your list for #1?

   Emphasize that it is important to pay attention to needs and personality when considering a career.

2. Explore group members' attitudes about needing to find a career direction before high school graduation. Ask the following questions:

   ▶ How important do you think it is to know what you want to do with your life before you leave high school?

   ▶ What have your parents and teachers told you about finding direction?

   ▶ How much are you worrying about finding a career for yourself?

   Encourage the students to continue to explore career options, but to relax about needing to find *the* direction while still in middle school/junior high or high school. Even during college, they can afford to delay commitment to a major for a few semesters and even change their major later. Encourage them to keep their options open and to expect to consider new possibilities during college. Professors, courses, and friends may give them new career ideas. Obviously, changes made late in college may necessitate going extra semesters, but the prospects of several decades in unsatisfying work make the investment of extra college time worth it. Remind them that it is not abnormal to change careers or pursue new directions within an area as an adult. For that reason, it is good to develop a broad base of knowledge, rather than a narrow range of technical skills. Abilities in reading, writing, and thinking will continue to be key factors in career success and adaptability.

3. If you have invited people from the community to visit your group, have the students interview them as a panel, asking these questions:

   ▶ How did you get to the career you have today? Was it a straight path?

   ▶ Which positions have been a good match for you, and which have not?

   ▶ What risks did you face in making career changes?

   ▶ What advice would you give to adolescents about career decisions?

   ▶ What educational or life experiences were most valuable for finding your career direction?

   ▶ Who or what influenced you regarding career choices along the way?

   ▶ What is most important to you now—money, status, or work satisfaction?

   ▶ Have your career positions allowed adequate time for family and a life outside your career?

   It is important to communicate that a person does not have to remain locked in a career groove for 40-plus years. That might relieve some of the group members' anxiety about finding the "perfect niche."

4. To introduce a new dimension, ask this question:

   ▶ Which do you think is more important—finding a satisfactory career, or finding a satisfactory relationship? Why?

   Suggest to the group that maybe they should make finding a satisfying career a higher priority than finding a satisfying relationship, given the impact of job dissatisfaction on relationships. Obviously that might not be a popular thought. However, it is also possible that the relationship might come through the career. Satisfaction in a career may reflect feeling in control of one's life. Certainly, satisfaction in the workplace contributes to general happiness. Making good academic choices, even in junior high or middle school, improves the chances of having options and career satisfaction later. Making poor choices for social reasons might close doors later.

5. Encourage them to set up their own brief career-shadowing experience, or do that as a group activity. You might devote a session to arranging a one-day (or half-day) experience for each individual. Each student could focus on one career, decide on a community location for the experience, and, with you, make arrangements (see "Important" below). They could then spend some time before the shadowing experience researching the career.

important

In my experience, it is best to have an adult make the call, in order to assure the professional that the career-shadowing experience will be relatively brief, that it will be supervised and prepared for, that only one student will be observing, and that he or she will be learning about a typical half or full day at work—including, perhaps, the sore feet, the fifty phone calls, the research, the long hours, the interruptions, and the stress (in other words, beyond the obvious). The person being shadowed needn't put on a show. Explain that the student would like to do a 15-minute interview sometime during the day about career preparation, career path, and career satisfaction. This length of experience is best for older adolescents, since it can demand stamina and a long attention span, and since professionals can probably communicate more comfortably about the realities of the work day to an older student. It is good to remember that a busy professional's day might be somewhat constrained by having someone "at the elbow," and that a service is being done. Stress to the students that they be on time, dress appropriately, be attentive, and thank their mentor. It is also important that both you and the student send a written thank-you after the experience.

6. For closure, have group members create a one-line bit of advice for themselves. Remind them that it is wise to keep their options open and to gain broad-based education and experience, while at the same time paying attention to themselves and to pertinent career information. Collect and dispose of the questionnaires—or encourage students to take these particular questionnaires home with them, for possible reference in the future.

choosing a career

1. List any and all career possibilities that you have considered in the past year: _____
   _____
   _____

2. Check any of the following that describe you accurately:

   ☐ like to be around people
   ☐ like to deal with writing
   ☐ like to work with my hands
   ☐ like to help people
   ☐ like to research, find out things
   ☐ like to feel a sense of contributing to the world
   ☐ like to work outdoors, not indoors
   ☐ like to put things in order

   ☐ like to deal with machines
   ☐ like creative, non-conforming activity
   ☐ like rules and regulations
   ☐ like to deal with scientific ideas
   ☐ like to perform in front of people
   ☐ like to deal with "fine print," details
   ☐ like to teach others new things

   ☐ like to sell things or ideas
   ☐ like to deal with data, numbers
   ☐ like to figure out how things work
   ☐ like to meet new people
   ☐ like to "get my hands dirty"
   ☐ like to make beautiful things, or make things beautiful
   ☐ like to construct, build things

3. Circle the 2-5 personal needs which will probably be important to you in a career:

   independence, making my own decisions

   to finish, not to have many unfinished strands

   order

   a sense of play

   achievement, rewards

   being the center of attention

   travel

   contact with people

   being in charge

   helping/guiding others

   to be done every day when leaving work

   predictability; knowing what to expect

   belonging to a group

   guidance from others

   advancement; going up the career ladder

   flexible schedule

   maternity/paternity leave

   a quiet, calm environment

   variety every day

   adequate time to be a parent

   living close to my extended family

   deadlines

   adventure and excitement

   an urban setting

   teamwork; working in a group

   solitude

   many things happening at once

4. How firm is your career direction right now? _____

5. Are you listening mostly to yourself or to others regarding career possibilities?
   _____

6. What kind of lifestyle would you like to have as an adult? (Consider income level, possessions, recreation, location, etc.) _____
   _____

focus: the future
expectations and dream images

background

As children grow, they watch and listen to the adults around them. They hear themselves described, they hear assessments about their potential, and they listen as others dream their futures for them. Even at a young age, they imagine themselves in the work world. As they mature, these images change as a result of new awareness. But they continue to hear the messages coming from significant adults in their lives, some of whom are encouraging them in particular directions. Sometimes the messages conflict with the images they have of themselves, and sometimes that conflict produces stress.

This session provides a chance for teens to sort the messages, whether or not they are in conflict. It might be a rare opportunity to pay attention to, and find support for, independent thoughts and dreams. This discussion is probably most appropriate for older adolescents, but even for middle-school children—especially high-ability children who may feel expectations early—the focus can be important for thinking ahead and examining what they are hearing from others.

objectives

- Students project realistically into the future.
- They consider the impact of parents' and others' projections on their vision of the future.
- They affirm positive and helpful input from significant adults.
- They assess the potential for conflict with significant adults regarding career direction.

suggestions

1. Hand out copies of "Images of the Future" (page 178) and ask the students to fill out the questionnaire with brief responses, anonymously. Use the questionnaire to generate discussion. You might want to have each student "read down" the entire sheet, with the group listening for themes, potential areas of conflict, and points of agreement. Follow their comments with questions or comments of your own. Examples:

176

> If there seems to be no conflict between your vision for yourself and others' visions for you, does that mean you and they have paid attention to your needs and wishes?

> Is agreement about your future direction typical in your life?

> How much do you usually agree with the adults who advise you about lifestyle? Education? Location?

> How do you think such agreement (or disagreement) will affect your future?

> If there is conflict, how does it affect your relationship with parents or teachers?

> How difficult will it be to pay attention to yourself in finding your direction?

> What would be the risks of charting an independent course?

> How realistic or idealistic are your personal expectations?

> How realistic or idealistic are the expectations others have for you?

2. Focus on paying attention to dreams. Ask these questions:

> Do you have an interest that you passionately hope to pursue?

> How important is it to follow dreams?

> What would be your fantasy life?

Whatever direction the discussion takes, consider it productive if group members are honest about their personal wishes and self-assessment. Validate their feelings ("I can sense your strong feelings for that"; "That would obviously mean a lot to you.") That will help more than analyzing the content of their comments.

3. For closure, ask the group what thoughts and feelings they had during the questionnaire and discussion. Collect and dispose of the questionnaires.

images of the future

1. What were some of your earliest images of yourself as an adult? How did you picture yourself?
   _____
   _____

2. What kind of work did you see yourself doing? _____
   _____

3. Where did you imagine yourself living? _____
   _____

4. If your parents or guardians have told you how they imagine you in the future, how old were you
   when they began to do that? _____

5. What did teachers suggest to you early in school about your future? _____
   _____

6. What have teachers suggested to you recently about your future? _____
   _____

7. What have you been hearing lately from your family about their expectations of you? _____
   _____

8. Who else in your life is giving you ideas for your future (boyfriend, girlfriend, other peers,
   religious/spiritual leader, a boss at work, etc.)? _____
   _____
   What are they saying? _____
   _____

9. Have adults in your life generally been supportive of you as they talk about your future? _____
   _____

10. Are your wishes and dreams for yourself generally in agreement with wishes and dreams others
    have for you? _____
    If so, what effect does that have on you? _____
    _____
    If not, what effect does that have on you? _____
    _____

11. What level of education will you need to pursue your goals? _____
    _____

focus: the future
attitudes about work

background

Although the key aspects of the preceding two sessions are appropriate for non-college-bound students, those students may feel that the ideas of career and college or other special training don't apply to them for a variety of reasons. This session is therefore meant to be appropriate for all students, and it is meant to provide a chance for all, no matter what their prospects may be, to discuss the world of work, attitudes toward work, and the meaning of work in their lives.

Even those who foresee only low-paying jobs for themselves in the near future will benefit from this discussion. This session can also encourage realistic thinking about individual self-sufficiency, especially regarding child-rearing, given the probability that many students will experience divorce and/or single parenthood. If you choose to omit the preceding two sessions, "Making Career Choices" and "Expectations and Dream Images," perhaps you can incorporate into this session some of the content that raises self-awareness about personality uniquenesses, skills, and personal needs in regard to work. The hope is that ultimately *all* group members will find a good fit, and personal satisfaction, in the workplace.

objectives

- Students assess their attitudes about work.
- They learn that what is said about work by family members, the media, and others has an impact on a person's attitude about work.
- They realize that there are many ways to feel about work.
- They realize that work has value in itself.

suggestions

1. Ask the students to define "work." Expect their definitions to vary. Then ask these questions:

   - Does work have to involve pay?
   - Does it have to take place outside the home?
   - What is your view of work that people do in a home office, such as for home-based businesses? Are there differences between that work and work that is done in a place of business elsewhere? Are they equal?

179

> Should the attitude toward household work, such as cooking, cleaning, and washing clothes, be different from the attitude toward work done outside the home or in a home office?

> Can money-earning work be *fun*—enjoyable? Who do you know who obviously enjoys, and has fun doing, money-earning work?

> Can other work be enjoyable—even household chores?

> How important is work in feeling satisfied about life?

> How do the media portray work—positively, negatively, rewarding, important? Can you think of examples from television programs, movies, newspapers?

> What is your attitude about the work that volunteers do in providing services to others? Do you see that as work? (You might mention that the United States has a somewhat unique, and long, tradition of volunteerism, which many community institutions depend on.)

> Do you think it is work if someone pursues a personal interest or project and invests many, many hours in it, with no thought of pay?

2. Ask the group to tell how they feel about work in general. Encourage them to elaborate, challenge each other, and communicate honestly. After they have expressed themselves, ask the following:

> How important is a person's attitude in making work satisfying?

> Do feelings about work have an effect on the family? If so, how?

> Do you think that negative and positive attitudes about work can become "habits"? Can you give examples of negative-attitude habits? Positive-attitude habits?

> How can people improve their attitudes about work? (Use positive self-talk; not fight against necessary work; be rested, alert, and pleasant to co-workers; enjoy the social aspect of work, when others are involved.)

> What can work do for a person? (Provide wages, occupy time, provide social contact, contribute to society, give one a sense of pride for doing something well, etc.)

3. Hand out copies of "The World of Work" (page 182) and ask the students to complete the questionnaire with brief responses, anonymously. Explain that they are to complete the list of significant adults (which may include anyone who has had an influence on their life), identify each person's workplace and position, and make a brief statement about the person's attitude toward work. If group members have had mostly negative role models regarding work satisfaction, ask them to brainstorm ways to overcome that influence. Then use the questionnaire as a springboard for discussion. Ask these questions:

> Do you expect work to be a big part of your adult life?

▶ Do you expect to work more than eight hours per day outside the home?

▶ How can you help yourself to have satisfaction in your work?

▶ What kinds of things can keep someone from feeling satisfied with a job? (A previous session, "Making Career Choices," emphasizes paying attention to personal needs in finding a career or job path. You may want to refer back to that session, if your group has already covered it.)

4. For closure, ask one or a few to summarize what has been discussed. Did the discussion cause them to think about work in a new way? If so, how? What do they think is the most important aspect of working? Might that differ from person to person? Collect and dispose of the questionnaires.

the world of work

significant adult	workplace and position	attitude toward work
1. Mother		
2. Father		
3. Grandmother		
4. Grandfather		
5. Teacher		
6. Aunt		
7. Uncle		
8.		
9.		
10.		
11.		
12.		

Have most of the significant adults in your life been positive, or negative, about their work?

_____

_____

Have most of them found satisfaction in their work? _____

For those who have felt good about their work, what seems to have been the main reason for their satisfaction? _____

_____

_____

For those who have not felt good about their work, what seems to have been the main reason for their dissatisfaction? _____

_____

_____

focus: the future
meaningful work

background

Many students may graduate from high school after little or no thoughtful adult input about planning for the future. Perhaps their parents and relatives are ill-equipped to provide guidance, for a variety of reasons. Their school counselor, probably with the typical too-large student load, may have been able to arrange only a brief annual check-in with the student, and even a meeting during the senior year might have come at a time when the student couldn't, or wouldn't, think about the future. Even though some older adolescents may have received little or no vocational guidance in the past, it is not too late to focus on the working world and assess their needs and options. If you are a school counselor, the suggestions for this session might be helpful for doing career planning with individuals or with groups.

This session is intended for non-college-bound older adolescents. It appears late in this series, and in this book, but it could certainly be used earlier in the life of a group, along with "Making Career Choices" and/or "Attitudes about Work," for taking stock of the self and of work options in planning for the future.

important

Even if you are not in a school setting, this would be a good time to invite a school counselor or someone from a vocational/trade school to make a presentation, answer questions about vocational/trade schools, and discuss other options for students who are not planning to go to college or university. Prior to inviting a speaker, take time during a preceding session to ask the students what they feel frustrated about in terms of planning for the future, what they would like to know more about, what they have already done, and what others have told them. You might even write down their specific questions and concerns and give them to the speaker in advance. Encourage the speaker to talk about various assessments that might be given (or that are already in the students' school files), to assist them in finding direction, and to help them find a good match in employment. Perhaps it is possible to pull out various assessment results for the group to look at during the session, with options noted for each individual. Financial aid can be discussed, and those who have already made plans for job training or immediate employment might share what they have learned about the process of establishing a direction and finding financial and other assistance.

If you plan to use suggestion #1, and if you did not previously use the "Making Career Choices" session, adapt the "Choosing a Career" handout (page 175) to fit your group, including appropriate items, in preparation for this session.

objectives

- Students learn about non-college options.
- They think about their strengths and limitations and consider possibilities for meaningful work.

suggestions

1. Find out what kinds of work experience group members have already had. Ask these questions:

   ▶ What kinds of part-time jobs have you had in the past—including very short-term jobs, such as helping a neighbor fix something, or doing a regular household chore?

   ▶ What kinds of duties did you enjoy the most in each part-time job?

   ▶ What did you enjoy the least in each one?

2. Hand out copies of "Choosing a Career" (page 175, your adapted version; see "Important" above) and ask the students to fill out the questionnaire with brief responses, anonymously. Invite each student to "read down" the entire sheet, with the group listening for potential fits between the reader's dreams and personality and personal needs.

   Respect individual situations and goals, and offer to find out additional information for them if that would help. Inform the group members about resources they can take advantage of in the counseling office, the school library, the community library, or elsewhere in the community. Arrange to introduce them to counselors or librarians, if that would be helpful and if it is possible.

3. If you did not already use the "Making Career Choices" session, you might incorporate suggestion #5 on career-shadowing here (see page 174).

4. For closure, ask one, a few, or all to comment on how ready they feel to leave school and enter full-time employment. In the event that some say they are thinking of dropping out of school, remind them that a diploma will improve their chances of finding employment. Encourage them to talk to you individually or to some other specific person (not just "to someone") about ways to overcome whatever obstacles seem to be standing in the way of their staying in school. Make appointments to talk more with the students yourself, or help them to arrange to talk with others, if possible.

focus: the future
college concerns

Many students with enough ability to succeed in college do not know much about college. Some have no college-educated family members to learn from. Some, because of their family's low socioeconomic level, assume that college is not possible for them. Some, even when their families are highly educated, are poorly informed about college particulars, but do not ask basic questions because they don't want to appear "stupid." They wonder about the terminology:

major	liberal arts
minor	orientation
credit hour	core course (or whatever an institution calls its required courses)
fraternity/sorority	
advisor	quiet dorms (or whatever term is applied to housing for serious students)
work study	
five-year program	

They wonder about other things as well:

where students study	what the typical adjustment problems are
how roommates are selected	
where medical help is available	differences between public and private colleges
if a student can change majors	
how accessible professors are	differences between large and small colleges
where students can get academic help	differences between colleges in big cities and in small towns
how students find their way around	financial aid possibilities
what constitutes success in college	how teaching, testing, and studying styles differ from high school
what the level of competition is	whether a person needs to have "direction" before going to college

185

This session can let them ask such basic questions.

Students who have adequate ability for college work, but feel they do not have enough money to go to college, should be encouraged to find out about financial aid—and to check out a variety of institutions, including nearby community colleges. Many institutions are concerned about keeping enrollments up, and some readily develop workable financial packages for those with ability. Today, too, a great number of young adults delay college, or spread it out over several years, and are employed throughout. This session can encourage those with high ability not to give up on the idea of higher education.

For students whose parents' dream is to have them accepted by a prestigious institution, there might be more interest in the "wedding" than the "marriage"—i.e., great attention is paid to the process of getting into college, but very little is given to preparing for the social and emotional dimensions of college life, which often is the key to surviving the first year. Sometimes even students with high intellectual ability, adequate financing, and good high school records are not successful during that critical period.

This session can help to prepare all students for the inevitable adjustments of college. It can also help to relieve anxiety in those who are concerned about not having a major in mind yet. And it can teach the vocabulary of college and university life.

important

This session requires advance preparation. It should be scheduled for a time when concerns about college, high-school course selection, or college applications are being expressed. Just prior to the Thanksgiving holiday break is an ideal time for seniors who are thinking about applications. In addition, first-year college students will probably arrive home for break before your school or institution dismisses and will be available to visit your group.

Invite a panel of 4–6 college students to be interviewed by you and your students. Try to have a variety—from large and small colleges and from a variety of socioeconomic, family, and high-school-success situations. You might also include someone attending a local or area community college.

Sometime before the session, ask your group to write down questions they have about college, anonymously—about schedules, dormitory living, orientation, courses, academic terminology, private vs. public institutions, costs, financial aid, etc. Collect the questions and have them ready.

If you choose not to invite a panel of college students, you might, of course, address these concerns yourself. Find out, first, what group members know about various aspects of college, and then fill in the gaps, perhaps at the next meeting, either with your own knowledge and experience or with information from people with recent or current college experience.

186

objectives

- Students learn college terminology.
- They learn about college life and the adjustments that most students have to make.
- They learn that financial aid might make college possible for those without great financial resources.

suggestions

1. Interview the college students, using the questions your group prepared earlier, some of the ideas mentioned in "Background," and new questions you invite from your group. You might also pursue some of these directions:

   - experiences with homesickness, illness, loneliness, finding friends
   - adjustments to fewer and new kinds of tests, less teacher feedback, heavy reading assignments, mid-term pressures, a new level of competition, extent of preparation needed for exams, rapid pace of courses, note-taking
   - adjustment to roommates
   - social life, comfort level, relaxing, finding people to eat with at the outset, getting along in a dormitory
   - size of institution (as related to feeling a sense of identity), finding friends, variety of cultures, access to professors, getting academic help, distance between classes
   - food, weight gain, illnesses, fatigue, sleeping in noisy dormitories
   - self-discipline and adjustments to less or more structure in life
   - time management: balancing jobs, social life, studying
   - money: how much is enough; budgeting; miscellaneous expenses; books
   - personal adjustments to other cultures and lifestyles
   - taking advantage of speakers, programs, campus events, campus groups
   - which high school courses gave good preparation
   - grades
   - financial aid processes
   - deciding on a major
   - if their institution is a good fit for them
   - personal growth and maturity (when, and in what ways, has it been noticed)
   - personal changes, in order to adjust
   - what colleges they looked at, and how they managed the process of college selection.

2. For closure, ask group members what was most helpful about this session. What feelings do they have when they think of college?

focus: the future
when and if i'm a parent

Many adolescents spend much of their time being angry at their parents, chafing under their restraints, and longing for independence. Yet, in most cases, because of basic realities in our society, they remain dependent on them for shelter, food, clothing, and financial support. That tug-and-pull produces conflict, which sometimes escalates dangerously. But it is the parents' job to provide support and to set limits on behavior. These tasks are important, and parents' competence and consistency in performing them have great impact. However, even when parents perform their tasks wisely, there is potential for conflict, and conflict might not stop when children leave home. Even at mid-life, "children" sometimes are still doing battle with their parents.

This session gives students a chance to talk about parent-adolescent issues. Even if some believe they never want to have children or even marry, they can still be involved in a discussion of parenting as if they will become parents someday, since the discussion will inevitably deal with how they themselves have been parented. What do group members hope they will never do as parents—and will always do? This session gives them the opportunity to share important feelings about their present life as they communicate about parenting.

If there are members of your group who already are parents, their opinions and feelings can be extremely valuable in the discussion, and the session might be especially helpful to them. They are undoubtedly already aware of some of the difficulties of parenting.

objectives

- Students learn to articulate feelings about the parenting they have experienced.
- They look ahead to the future while assessing their own past experiences.
- They think about their personality styles, beliefs, and values as they imagine themselves as parents.

1. Begin by having the students define "parenting." Then proceed with broad questions like these:

   ▶ What is the "job," or responsibilities, of a parent?

   ▶ When does parenting begin? When does it end?

2. Generate discussion with some of the following questions:

   ▶ What is difficult about parenting?

   ▶ What is important in parenting very young children?

   ▶ What are some typical conflicts between parents and children?

   ▶ What conflicts are probably part of the separation process that happens during adolescence? (Conflicts about privacy, curfews, clothes, friends, choices, direction, achievement, appearance, etc.)

   ▶ What makes parenting an adolescent particularly difficult? (Perhaps the sense of having less control as the teen moves more and more into the world beyond the family and establishes his or her own identity?)

   ▶ What kinds of fears and anxieties do parents probably have about their children?

   ▶ How much independence is appropriate for an adolescent?

   ▶ What are the challenges of step-parenting?

   ▶ What is the most important positive quality in a parent? (Expect many possible answers.)

3. Encourage the group to look realistically into the future by asking these questions:

   ▶ What will you be like as an adult? Give 3–5 adjectives that you think might fit you someday. (If students have difficulty here, suggest some of the following as starters.)

restless	patient	consistent
settled	impatient	inconsistent
moving often	long-suffering	taking time for children
contented	tolerant	
tense	critical	not taking time for children
conflict-ridden	stable	
serene	unstable	lazy
calm	wise	workaholic
"hyper"	impulsive	balanced regarding work and play

4. Continue the discussion by asking the following:

   ▶ What have you learned from your parent(s) about how to parent or how not to parent?

▶ How will you want to be like your parent(s) in parenting style?

▶ How will you want to be different from your parent(s) in parenting style?

▶ When, in a marriage, is a good time to begin having children?

Mention that our own parenting behaviors often reflect the ways our parents behaved with us, especially when they were (and we are) under stress. We model their behaviors, even if we were convinced that we would never behave as they did with us. Then assure the group that we can change those patterned behaviors through insight and effort. We have choices. If we understand ourselves, we are more likely to choose wisely. Many communities offer parenting workshops to help parents become more effective at the job of parenting.

5. For closure, ask the students for comments about what they are thinking or feeling, now that the discussion of future parenting is finished. Tell them that they don't have to be perfect parents, just caring and responsible parents—if they choose to be parents.

final sessions

final sessions
planning ahead: wish lists

As a group nears the end of a series, especially at the end of a school year, members may bring up serious matters for the first time. Some may have waited a long time to feel safe enough to ask for advice about a personal situation or to check out group reaction to a personal concern. Others may still not feel comfortable enough to mention something in the group, but will arrange to speak with the leader individually. In order not to close the door on such needs, while still preparing the group for closure, it is wise to let the year wind down with increasingly relaxing and comfortable topics. This one is meant to be light. It encourages group members to "cap" ongoing concerns, prepare to terminate as a group, and look ahead.

objectives

- Students assess both past and present by making wish lists.
- They express sincere personal wishes.

suggestions

1. Remind the group that the series of discussions, and perhaps their group, are nearly done. It is important to state that directly. Explain that this session is meant to help them prepare for ending. Introduce the topic by encouraging them to think back over some of their personal discussion "themes." Ask these questions:

   ▶ What ideas and thoughts did you mention more than once?

   ▶ What thoughts kept coming up for you, whether or not you mentioned them?

   ▶ Which issues and problems have stayed the same during the entire time the group has met, and which have changed?

   ▶ What personal issues have been resolved, taken care of?

   ▶ What issues and problems will likely continue to be in your thoughts in the future?

   ▶ What issues and themes do you remember hearing from others in the group?

2. Ask them to think of endings to the following sentence stems, and then go around the group, with each student finishing both stems:

192

"I used to wish for..."

"Now I wish for...."

Explain that "I used to wish for..." can refer to any time in life. They can list many wishes for each sentence stem. After hearing from everyone, encourage the group to add as many more "used to wish/now I wish" combinations as they want to, offering them whenever they come to mind.

3. Address the differences between "young" and "older" wishes. What has contributed to the differences? What has changed?

4. Invite the students to share other current wishes for their own lives, their families, or their friends. They might later share wishes for their community, nation, or the world. They might also make wishes for various members of the group, based on concerns heard during the life of the group.

5. For closure, affirm their wishes as good wishes, and convey to them that you hope their wishes will come true. If the next meeting will be the last one, remind them of that, and ask if there are any wishes or recommendations for making it a memorable and proper ending (food, music, and autographs, perhaps?).

final sessions
an informal assessment

background

To conclude a series of sessions, one last questionnaire is offered here. It should be fairly easy for students to complete, and the group will enjoy hearing one another's creative, honest, and thoughtful comments. This can be a good, upbeat way to end a year (or shorter series) of group discussions. The sentence stems on the questionnaire look back or look ahead. Some of them might generate discussion. The questionnaire can also be used as a light break at any time during a series of sessions.

For additional thoughts and suggestions on bringing your group to a close, see "Endings" on page 17.

objectives

- Students feel a sense of closure to their discussion experience.
- They interact with one another in a positive way.

suggestions

1. Hand out copies of "An Informal Assessment" (page 196) and ask the students to write brief endings to the sentence stems. Invite them to be honest and serious, clever, critical, sentimental, or all of those, but they should, as always, communicate meaningfully. Remind them that you have respected their ability to speak honestly and sincerely, and you assume they will want to do that here, too. They can be honest to whatever extent is comfortable for them. Tell them that the assessment is meant to help them look backward and look forward.

2. Have the students read down their lists. If a particular item generates discussion, pursue it. Keep in mind, however, that all group members should have a chance to share their lists during the session.

3. If this is the final group meeting, encourage the students to share what they feel they have gained through the group experience. They can do this orally or in writing. Written summaries can be valuable personal feedback for a leader, since they give group members a chance to express private thoughts. This is one time where it is appropriate for them to identify themselves by name, since this is personal communication to you as facilitator. Assure them of confidentiality. As an alternative to this suggestion, see Suggestion #5 below.

In addition, if it might be helpful and necessary for building support for discussion groups in your setting or district, invite the students to add a sentence for administrators or brochures, expressing the value of the group experience for them. Assure them that these statements will remain anonymous.

4. Encourage the students to talk about ending the group. This is perhaps the most important suggestion in this session, since endings are difficult for many people. Talking about feelings at this point is an important part of the group process. Ask these questions:

   ▶ What does it feel like to know that this is our final meeting?

   ▶ Are endings usually easy or difficult for you? Can you recall an example or two?

5. As an alternative to Suggestion #3 above, hand out copies of "Discussion Group Evaluation" (page 197). Either have group members fill out the evaluation during this session, or ask them to return it to you the next day. Emphasize that you want their honest responses and opinions. Point out that they should not sign this form—it is meant to be anonymous.

6. For closure, tell the group you are glad they committed themselves to the discussion group, took it seriously, became a group, or whatever else is appropriate. Thank them for their special contributions to the group. Wish them well.

Use your own judgment about collecting and destroying the "An Informal Assessment" handouts. Group members might like to keep them as souvenirs and to look back at them sometime in the future.

an informal assessment

Finish as many of the sentence stems as you can or wish to.

1. I'm working on _____.

2. I'll probably _____.

3. I will know I am grown up when I _____.

4. My most irrational fear about the future is _____.

5. Some advice I'm going to follow is_____.

6. I wish I knew more about _____.

7. I wish everybody would understand that I_____.

8. My future fantasy is_____.

9. My parents will probably be happy if I_____.

10. A beautiful memory I will always have is_____.

11. I hope I never have to _____.

12. Someday I'll _____.

13. I should thank (should have thanked)_____.

14. I still can't tolerate_____.

15. Where have I been in my life? My past has been _____.

16. Where am I heading in my life? My future will be_____.

17. I'm glad I was part of this group because _____.

I know I don't have to be perfect.

I understand that life is a process, and there is no "finished product."

Life instructs.

I am not done learning.

discussion group evaluation

What did you think of the discussion group experience? Your feedback is important! Your honest—and anonymous—responses will help future groups. Please complete and return this evaluation form. Thank you for your time.

1. Circle the number that best describes how you would rate each of the following.

   1 = excellent; 2 = good; 3 = average; 4 = fair; 5 = poor.

   1 2 3 4 5   The group experience as a whole.

   1 2 3 4 5   The ability of the leader to guide the group.

   1 2 3 4 5   The warmth and concern of the group leader.

   1 2 3 4 5   The leader's respect for every member of the group.

   1 2 3 4 5   The value of the group for people like me.

   1 2 3 4 5   The value of the group for me personally.

   1 2 3 4 5   The general level of comfort and emotional/personal safety in the group for sharing feelings.

   1 2 3 4 5   The level of comfort and safety I felt in the group personally.

   1 2 3 4 5   The respect I felt for the other members of my group.

   1 2 3 4 5   The respect that the other members of my group showed toward me.

2. Which topics were most interesting and helpful for you? _____

   _____

   _____

   _____

   _____

3. I would/wouldn't recommend this group to a friend because: _____

   _____

   _____

   _____

4. Additional comments: _____

   _____

   _____

   _____

index

about the author

Jean Sunde Peterson, Ph.D., taught for many years in Iowa, Minnesota, South Dakota, and Berlin, Germany, before her doctoral work in counseling and human development. For the past several years she has conducted workshops and consulted with schools about underachievement, discussion groups, multicultural issues, listening skills for teachers, and the social and emotional concerns of high-ability students. During her many years in South Dakota, she was also an adjunct faculty member at Augustana College in English and foreign-language teaching methodology, and created summer language camps for children there. She is the author of *Talk with Teens about Self and Stress* (Free Spirit Publishing, 1993), several small textbooks and teaching guides, and many articles and chapters dealing with English and foreign language teaching, counseling, and gifted education. She is also the author of a collection of poems, *Gifted at Risk*. The former South Dakota Teacher of the Year developed discussion groups for adolescents in Sioux Falls and later employed that format as a counselor in middle schools and alternative-school and substance-abuse-treatment facilities. She is currently on the faculty in Counseling and Development at Purdue University.

Other Great Books from Free Spirit

Talk with Teens About Self and Stress
50 Guided Discussions for School and Counseling Groups
by Jean Sunde Peterson, Ph.D.
Fifty guided discussions help students share their feelings and concerns, gain self-awareness and self-esteem, cope with stress, anticipate and solve problems, and more. Includes 20 reproducible handout masters. For grades 7–12.
$19.95; 192 pp.; softcover; 8½" x 11"

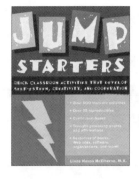

Jump Starters
Quick Classroom Activities That Develop Self-Esteem, Creativity, and Cooperation
by Linda Nason McElherne, M.A.
Make the most of every minute in your classroom by keeping this book close at hand. Features fifty-two themes within five topics: Knowing Myself, Getting to Know Others, Succeeding in School, Life Skills, and Just for Fun. Includes reproducible handout masters. For teachers, grades 3–6.
$21.95; 184 pp.; softcover; illus.; 8½" x 11"

Challenging Projects for Creative Minds
12 Self-Directed Enrichment Projects That Develop and Showcase Student Ability for Grades 1–5
by Phil Schlemmer, M.Ed., and Dori Schlemmer
The best way to prepare children for the future is to teach them how to learn, and that's just what these projects do. Each project sparks kids' imaginations, calls on their creativity, and challenges them to solve problems, find and use information, and think for themselves. For teachers, grades 1–5.
$29.95; 144 pp.; softcover; illus.; 8½" x 11"

Teaching Gifted Kids in the Regular Classroom
Strategies and Techniques Every Teacher Can Use to Meet the Academic Needs of the Gifted and Talented
by Susan Winebrenner
The definitive guide to meeting the learning needs of gifted students in the mixed-abilities classroom—without losing control, causing resentment, or spending hours preparing extra material. Written by a teacher and field-tested, this book makes school more rewarding for everyone. Includes 30 reproducible handout masters. For teachers, all grades.
$21.95; 168 pp.; softcover; 8½" x 11"

Challenging Projects for Creative Minds
20 Self-Directed Enrichment Projects That Develop and Showcase Student Ability for Grades 6 & Up
by Phil Schlemmer, M.Ed., and Dori Schlemmer
Give your students opportunities to explore beyond core curriculum by completing in-depth projects that promote lifelong learning skills. Reproducible forms help students choose and plan a project, report their progress and problems, keep a record of their work time, and evaluate the project after completion. For teachers, grades 6 & up.
$34.95; 168 pp.; softcover; illus.; 8½" x 11"

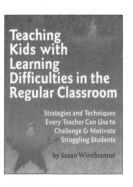

Teaching Kids with Learning Difficulties in the Regular Classroom
Strategies and Techniques Every Teacher Can Use to Challenge & Motivate Struggling Students
by Susan Winebrenner
Proven, practical teaching methods, strategies, and techniques for meeting the needs of special education students, those labeled "slow" or "remedial," and all others who struggle to learn in the mixed-abilities classroom. For teachers, all grades.
$27.95; 248 pp.; softcover; 8½" x 11"

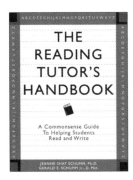

The Reading Tutor's Handbook

A Commonsense Guide to Helping Students Read and Write

by Jeanne Shay Schumm, Ph.D., and Gerald E. Schumm Jr., D. Min.

Based on Jeanne Schumm's years of experience training volunteer tutors, this book is for anyone who wants to make a difference in a young person's life. Includes reproducible handout masters. For grades 1–12.

$18.95; 152 pp.; softcover; 8½" x 11"

Sexual Harassment and Teens

A Program for Positive Change

by Susan Strauss with Pamela Espeland

A timely, comprehensive program that addresses the causes, effects, and laws concerning sexual harassment; examines school policies; presents case studies; describes procedures for preventing harassment; and more. Includes resources. For teachers, grades 7–12.

$17.95; 160 pp.; softcover; 8½" x 11"

Growing Good Kids

28 Activities to Enhance Self-Awareness, Compassion, and Leadership

by Deb Delisle and Jim Delisle, Ph.D.

Created by teachers and classroom-tested, these fun and meaningful enrichment activities build children's skills in problem solving, decision making, cooperative learning, divergent thinking, and communication. For grades 4–8.

$21.95; 168 pp.; softcover; illus.; 8½" x 11"

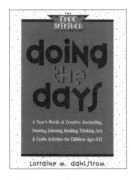

TNT Teaching

Over 200 Dynamite Ways to Make Your Classroom Come Alive

written and illustrated by Randy Moberg

Dozens of fresh, exciting ways to present the curriculum, plus new uses for media equipment—even a course in cartooning. A wonderful resource for your Free Spirited Classroom. For teachers, grades K–8.

$19.95; 160 pp.; softcover; illus.; 8½" x 11"

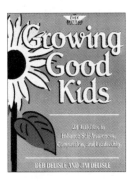

The Bully Free Classroom

Over 100 Tips and Strategies for Teachers K–8

by Allan L. Beane, Ph.D.

Positive and practical, this solution-filled book can make any classroom a place where all students are free to learn without fear. It spells out 100 proven strategies teachers can start using immediately. Includes true stories, checklists, resources, and reproducible handout masters. For teachers, grades K–8.

$19.95; 176 pp.; softcover; 8½" x 11"

Doing the Days

A Year's Worth of Creative Journaling, Drawing, Listening, Reading, Thinking, Arts & Crafts Activities for Children Ages 8–12

by Lorraine Dahlstrom

A total of 1,464 fun learning activities linked to the calendar year. Spans all areas of the curriculum and stresses whole language, cooperative learning, and critical thinking skills. For teachers, grades 3–6.

$21.95, 240 pp.; softcover; illus.; 8½" x 11"

Teach to Reach

Over 300 Strategies, Tips, and Helpful Hints for Teachers of All Grades

by Craig Mitchell with Pamela Espeland

A classroom teacher shares hundreds of "tricks of the trade"—ideas to help all teachers sharpen their skills, enhance the learning environment, and make school more enjoyable for everyone. For teachers, all grades.

$9.95; 208 pp.; softcover; 5⅛" x 6"

Up from Underachievement

How Teachers, Students, and Parents Can Work Together to Promote Student Success

by Diane Heacox, Ph.D.

This step-by-step program helps students of all ages, with all kinds of school problems, to break the failure chain. Students are motivated to succeed because they are part of the team. Includes reproducible handout masters. For parents and teachers of all grades.

$16.95; 144 pp.; softcover; 8½" x 11"

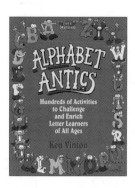

Alphabet Antics

Hundreds of Activities to Challenge and Enrich Letter Learners of All Ages
written and illustrated by Ken Vinton, M.A.
This fresh, inventive approach to the ABCs promotes creativity, stimulates curiosity, and invites exploration and discovery through activities and illustrated, reproducible handouts. For grades K–6.
$19.95; 144 pp.; softcover; illus.; 8½" x 11"

Making the Most of Today

Daily Readings for Young People on Self-Awareness, Creativity, & Self-Esteem
by Pamela Espeland and Rosemary Wallner
Quotes from figures including Eeyore, Mariah Carey, and Dr. Martin Luther King Jr. guide you through a year of positive thinking, problem solving, and practical lifeskills—the keys to making the most of every day. For ages 11 & up.
$9.95; 392 pp.; softcover; 4¼" x 6¼"

Write from the Edge

A Creative Borders Book
written and illustrated by Ken Vinton, M.A.
Fifty witty, wacky illustrated border pages promote creativity, self-expression, and divergent thinking. Includes project ideas, discussion questions, and thought-provoking quotations. All fifty border pages are reproducible. For teachers, grades K–6.
$19.95; 120 pp.; softcover; illus.; 8½" x 11"

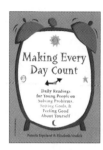

Making Every Day Count

Daily Readings for Young People on Solving Problems, Setting Goals, & Feeling Good About Yourself
by Pamela Espeland and Elizabeth Verdick
Each entry in this book of daily readings begins with a thought-provoking quotation, followed by a brief essay and a positive "I"-statement that relates the entry to the reader's own life. For ages 11 & up.
$9.95; 392 pp.; softcover; 4¼" x 6¼"

Creating Portfolios For Success in School, Work, and Life

by Martin Kimeldorf
A portfolio is a powerful tool for learning, assessment, and self-discovery. The exercises in this hands-on book lead students through the process of preparing four different types of port-folios: personal, student, project, and professional. Includes reproducibles.
For ages 12 & up.
$11.95; 96 pp.; softcover; illus.; 8½" x 11"

Teacher's Guide
For teachers, grades 7 & up.
$12.95; 72 pp.; softcover; illus.; 8½" x 11"

Stick Up for Yourself!

Every Kid's Guide to Personal Power and Positive Self-Esteem
Revised and Updated
by Gershen Kaufman, Ph.D., Lev Raphael, Ph.D., and Pamela Espeland
Newly revised and updated, this is the ultimate resource for any kid who's ever been picked on, bossed around, or treated unfairly. Simple words and real-life examples show how children can stick up for themselves with other kids, big sisters and brothers, even grown-ups.
For ages 8–12.
$11.95; 128 pp.; softcover; illus.; 6" x 9"

Teacher's Guide
A 10-Part Course in Self-Esteem and Assertiveness for Kids
For teachers, grades 3–7.
$19.95; 128 pp.; softcover; 8½" x 11"

To place an order or to request a free catalog of SELF HELP FOR KIDS® and SELF–HELP FOR TEENS® materials, please write, call, email, or visit our Web site:

Free Spirit Publishing Inc.
400 First Avenue North • Suite 616 • Minneapolis, MN 55401-1724
toll-free 800.735.7323 • local 612.338.2068 • fax 612.337.5050
help4kids@freespirit.com • www.freespirit.com